Spurgeon's Sermons on Ruth

(Sermons on the Whole Bible)

Charles H. Spurgeon

Bibliographic Information

Charles H. Spurgeon (1834 – 1892), affectionately known by many as "the Prince of Preachers," addressed more than 10 million people during his ministry, baptized thousands of converts, and wrote so extensively and persuasively that his sermons have sold more than 50 million copies. Spurgeon's sermons were previously published in 1855 in a multi-volume series known as *The New Park Street Pulpit*.

an Ichthus Publications edition

Copyright © 2014 Ichthus Publications
ISBN 10: 1500974250
ISBN 13: 978-1500974251

www.ichthuspublications.com

CONTENTS

1 The Nature and Design of Divine Chastening   *5*
    A Sermon from 1 Corinthians 11:32 with Exposition from Ruth 1

2 Ruth Deciding for God   *22*
    A Sermon from Ruth 1:16

3 Ruth's Reward—or, Cheer for Converts   *39*
    A Sermon from Ruth 2:12

4 Mealtime In The Corn Fields   *57*
    A Sermon from Ruth 2:14

5 Spiritual Gleaning   *75*
    A Sermon from Ruth 2:15

6 A Sermon for Gleaners   *88*
    A Sermon from Ruth 2:15, 16

1
THE NATURE AND DESIGN OF DIVINE CHASTENING

"When we are judged, we are chastened of the Lord, that we should not be condemned with the world."

—1 Corinthians 11:32

THERE HAD BEEN GREAT irregularities in the Corinthian Church with regard to the Lord's Supper. They had made that solemn festival a scene of gluttony. Each person had brought his own provisions with him and while the rich were feasting on dainties, the poor often had scarcely anything to eat. The Apostle Paul tells them that on that occasion they did not come together for a feast of carnal things. He says, "In eating everyone takes before others his own supper, and one is hungry, and another is drunk. What? Have you not houses to eat and to drink in? Or despise you the Church of God, and shame them that have not? What shall I say to you? Shall I praise you in this? I praise you not."

Now, on account of these irregularities, God was pleased to visit the Church at Corinth with many sore afflictions. A great many of the members were smitten with sickness and some were even taken away by death. Little did the Church at Corinth understand the reason for this plague, this visitation of God upon their members, but the Apostle explains it to them. He says, "For this cause"—note the 30th verse—"many are weak and sickly among you, and many sleep. For if we would judge ourselves, we would not be judged." There is a constant judgment going on in the Church of God. If we would judge ourselves and walk orderly and worthily in God's sight, then we shall not be judged—the plagues will not come upon us. But when we are judged, what are we to say with regard to that? Is that a proof that God hates His Church and that He has cast His people away? And especially, too, if any die as the result of their iniquities, is that a proof that they perish eternally? "Oh no" says Paul, "they are judged now, in this world—they are chastened now of the Lord, that they should not be condemned with the world."

What a great mystery is Providence, even to us who believe in a future state! We throw down the gauntlet of defiance to the infidel. We declare and with the best reason on our side, that it is utterly impossible for men to understand how there can be any justice in the dispensations of God in this world, or how there can be any justice in God at all, if there is not a time to come in which the great mysteries of this life shall all be set right. We defy any man who disbelieves in the immortality of the soul, to account for the fact that the most godly are those who suffer the most, and that, often, those who have the greatest happiness in this world are the men who least deserve it and are the most wicked! If there is not a future state of rewards and punishments. If the just man shall not reap the full reward of all his sufferings and griefs, and if the wicked shall not receive punishment for all his sins, how can God be just—and how can the Judge of all the earth do right?

There is also another mistake into which we may very readily fall. It is very easy for us to judge of the characters of men by their position in this world—and so to judge in a manner entirely apart from the facts. Some will have it that if a man is exceedingly prosperous, it stands to reason that he must have been good. "Surely God would not have rewarded him," they say, "unless there had been something worthy about him." This is what is inculcated upon our children. How often does the father pat his child upon the head and, pointing to an alderman who is growing exceedingly fat with riches, tell his son that he must be a good boy and then he, too, will become as great? Or, taking him by the house of some exceedingly rich man, how often does the father tell his child that if he shall be good—which is, I suppose, but a brief, pithy expression, to signify if he shall be obedient and keep the Laws of God—then he shall be rich? And so, in

fact, it is thought impossible to make a child understand that a man may be rich and yet wicked—that he may be happy in this world and have much of visible blessedness and yet, after all, be a stranger to God and be the very reverse of good! We, I trust, in our riper years, are free enough from such a mistake as that.

Yes, Friends, we must never judge of men's inward condition by their outward position. A rich man may be gracious and a poor man may be wicked—and we may turn the truth in the other direction and declare that many are the poor who have Divine Grace within, and many are the rich who are but fattening for God's slaughtering-day at the last! It is a well-known fact, which has, doubtless, led to both the errors which I have mentioned—the error of thinking that God is unrighteous and also the error of judging men by their outward state. I say it is doubtless a fact that many of the true children of God are exceedingly troubled in this world, while, full often, the wicked escape. Why is this? Our text explains it. It declares that "we are chastened of the Lord, that we should not be condemned with the world."

I. THE PEOPLE OF GOD ARE CHASTENED OF THE LORD—THEY ARE MORE CHASTENED THAN ANY OTHER MEN. They are chastened every morning and they are plagued all the day long. Why is this? God must be right in acting thus—what is His reason? I will give you a few reasons. First, the righteous are more chastened than other men because their sins are worse than those of others. Secondly, they are more chastened than other men, that God may make them an example of His hatred against sin. And then, they also receive extraordinary chastening because of God's extraordinary value of them and His determination to wean them from their sins and cure them of their iniquities.

I say, in the first place, that God chastens His people more than others, and we may find a reason for this in the fact that their sins are worse than those of other men. I do not mean that they are outwardly worse—I will defend the character of the people of God from any such aspersion as that! I do not mean that the people of God are worse sinners than others, judged by the Law, weighed in the scales of the Justice which will try all men. It is in another respect that they are worse—not in the light of the Law of God, but in the light of the Gospel.

They are worse, partly because the righteous have more of the Light of God than other men. In proportion to the Light of God against which we sin, is the greatness of our iniquity. A sin which a Hottentot might commit and which God would wink at because of his ignorance, He would never pass by in His own children, because His children know better. They have spiritual discernment. They are not so foolish as to put bitter for sweet, and sweet for bitter. Their conscience has been enlightened and besides, they have the Word of God and the indwelling of the Spirit—and when they sin, they sin against greater light and knowledge than other men have. Hence it is that their sins stand in the very first position with regard to guilt. And what wonder, therefore, that God should sorely chasten them?

On this thought I will not lay greater stress, but pass on to observe that the sins of the righteous are worse than those of other men from the fact of the greater mercy which they have received. It is impossible for any man to sin so grievously against God as the man who is God's favorite. He who lies nearest to our bosom is capable of grieving us the most. Why is it that the sin of Judas was so great? It was because Judas was an Apostle and he had been a friend of Christ. Jesus might have said to him, "It was not an enemy that reproached Me; then I could have borne it. Neither was it he that hated Me that did magnify himself against Me; then I would have hid Myself from him. But it was you, a man My equal, My guide and My acquaintance. We took sweet counsel together and walked unto the House of God in company." Christ feels a blow from an enemy, but a stab from His friend is "the unkindest cut of all."

What? When Christ has chosen us out of the world and has redeemed us with His precious blood. When God has taken us into His family, when He has wrapped the righteousness of Christ about us, like a robe, and has promised us an eternal dwelling place at His right hand—shall we sin, do you think, and shall not our sin be counted to be a heinous offense, indeed, because of the love at which we kicked and the great mercy over which we stumbled? A husband feels an unkind word from his wife far more than from anyone else because he loves her better than he loves others and, therefore, she has the greater power to grieve him. And Christ cares little for all the railing of a wicked world, but if His Church speaks slightingly of Him—if she offends Him—then is He cut even to the heart! If we take anyone into our friendship, we entertain at once a jealousy of him. If he speaks evil behind our back, we say, "If you had been an enemy, I would never have noticed it. You might have said just what you chose, and I would never have rebuked you. But you professed to be my friend and if you say anything against me, I cannot bear it. This wounds me sorely and, therefore, I must rebuke you for it."

One good old writer says, "When the Lord takes a man to His private chamber and admits him into His secrets, He at once becomes jealous of him—He will not permit him to sin so deeply as others. 'Oh,' He says, 'have I made you My friend? Have I walked with you? Have I permitted you to lean your head upon My bosom and will you go away and break My Laws, and rebel against One who has been so loving to you as to admit you into the secret place of His Tabernacle? Then, surely, your sin is great, indeed, and I 'will chasten you for it.'" Beloved, if you will set your sins in this light, you will at once perceive that it is no wonder that God chastens you! Ah, Brothers and Sisters, when we think of the great mercy of God to us—of His overflowing kindness, both in Providence and Grace—when we meditate upon the fond affection which has cradled us from our youth up, and the strong protection that has guarded us from all harm, surely we must think that offenses against God, committed by us, are worse than the sins of other men who have never tasted of such mercies as those which we receive daily! This, also, is another proof of the greatness of the sin of God's people as compared with the sin of others—and is a reason for His chastising them.

Besides, my Friends, the sins of God's people are worse than those of other men from the ruinous effect of their example. When a worldling is seen drunk, there is sin, of course—but when a Church member is seen reeling in the streets, how much worse it is! The world makes this a grand excuse for itself. It is under the shadow of the imperfections of the Church that wicked men find shelter from the scorching heat of their conscience. If they can detect a minister in sin. If they can discover a deacon or an elder indulging in iniquity. If they can quote a justification for sin from the lips of a Church member, how content and pleased the wicked are! They did, as it were, but walk in their transgressions before— but when they find a Church member in the same path, then they run greedily in the way of iniquity! I say, Brothers and Sisters, our sins deserve twice the afflictions of other men if we rebel because they do more mischief. And often, you know, judges have to estimate transgressions not merely by their guilt, but by the influence of the example of the criminal—and so, God will the more heavily chasten His people because if they sin, they do so much damage to the morals of mankind and bring so much dishonor upon the name of the Lord their God! For all these reasons I am sure I am right in saying that the sins of God's people are, in God's esteem, worse than the sins of other men and, perhaps, this is one reason why He always chastens them, even when He lets the wicked go unpunished for a while. This is not, however, the grand reason. I come to another.

Why does God chasten His people while He permits so many others to go unpunished? I take it that another reason is that He may give a manifest and striking example of His hatred of sin. When God chastens all ordinary man for iniquity, His justice is seen. But when He lays His rod upon His own child, then at once you discover how much He hates iniquity. When Brutus condemned traitors, Rome could see his justice, but when his two sons are brought up and accused of the crime, and he says—"Lictors, do your duty. Strip and beat them." And after they have been scourged, when he bids them take them away and treat them as common malefactors, then all Rome is startled with the inflexibility of the justice of Brutus! So, when God smites His own children—when He lays the rod on those who are very dear to Him, when He makes them public examples—then even the world itself cannot withhold its admiration of the justice of God.

When David—the man after God's own heart—was smitten so sorely for one sin, God's justice was more fully manifested than in the punishment of a hundred ordinary men. There were many men, throughout Jerusalem, ten times worse than David, but they escaped Scot free. Not so David, because David was much loved of God and, therefore, he must be chastened that the whole world might see that God hates sin, even when it nestles in the breasts of His own beloved children. Never was there such a proof of God's hatred of iniquity as when He put His own Son to death! And next to that, the chastisement of His own well-beloved children is the most forcible proof of His hatred of iniquity. I take it that this is a second reason why the righteous are so much chastened.

But then the best reason is because of the high value which God sets upon His people. Our text says, "We are chastened of the Lord, that we should not be condemned with the world." God has a great esteem for His people and He will not let them perish. But He knows right well that if He allowed them to go unchastened, they would soon destroy themselves and lose their interest in His love. This He never can permit, for that were contrary to His oath and contrary to His Covenant. Therefore does He chasten them. So, whenever you are a chastened child of God, you may draw comfort from it. Samuel Rutherford, in writing to Lady Kenmure, who was in deep affliction, having first lost her two children and then her husband and mother, said, "Your Ladyship must certainly be a special favorite of Heaven, for if you were not, surely the Lord would not take all this pain to make you fit for Heaven. If He did not love you very much, He would not be so jealous of your love. For I take it," he said, "this is the reason why He took away those who were dear to you—because He would have every atom of your love and, therefore, would not permit anything to be spared to you upon which your heart was set."

As for the wicked, let them have what they please—let them set their hearts upon their riches, it is their only treasure—let them give their love to their lusts and to their carnal pleasures. God wants not their love—the love of the wicked is not pleasant to Him—He wants not their praises. What have they to do with loving and praising Him while they are reveling in their iniquities? But with regard to the righteous, God loves them—He wants their love and He will have it—and He will chasten them until He gets it. He will make them even as a weaned child, taking away the breasts of this world from their lips, and putting bitterness into their mouths till they begin to loathe this world and long for a better—long to leave their present state and to be with Him who is their All-in-All!

Besides, with regard to the wicked, God says of them, "Let them go on sinning, let them fill up the measure of their iniquities." A reprobate may be many years in sin before he is discovered or punished. You have known and seen, of late, in the commercial embezzlements of our time, how long a wicked and ungodly man may go on in sin. Year after year he is embezzling money, yet he is not found out. There are a thousand opportunities for discovery, but, somehow or other, his wickedness is masked and it seems as though Providence itself helped him to conceal his iniquity. But if you are a child of God, don't you try it, for you will be found out the first time! Mark that—an heir of Heaven can never go on long in villainy. God will straightway set him up as an object of scorn before men—and why? Because the Lord loves us and He does not want us to fill up the measure of our iniquity. He desires to stop us at once in our sin and, therefore, you will find this is a fact verified in your observation—if a child of God commits but a small act of dishonesty, it is certain to be found out—but an ungodly man may heap up his iniquities and yet go unpunished for many and many a day!

No, I will go further than that! Many a man has pursued a life of fornication and uncleanness and has never, at least as far as we can see, been punished or chastened. His life seems to have been a continued round of gaiety. He has gone from mirth to mirth, and from merriment to debauchery. He has been the envy of his fellow men, for the strength of his body and for the vigor of his health. He has even come to die and has gone to his grave softly, without a band in his death, or a pang in his last hour—and why is this? Simply because the Lord said, "Let him alone; he is joined to idols; let him go." God did not care to cast stumbling-blocks in his path. He was running his downward way and God left him alone. "There," He said, "let him work his own damnation. Let him run the downward road. I will not stop him." And, like the swine possessed with devils, that man has run violently down a steep place into the sea of damnation and has never discovered his lost state till he has perished in the fiery waters of Hell!

But you will not find the child of God go on like that. David grossly sinned once, but it was not long before he was chastened for it. Another man might have lived for years in adultery and yet not been punished. Not so with the Believer—he must be chastened at once. God will keep His people free from the growth of iniquity. As soon as the first weed springs up, He lays the hoe to its roots. But as for the wicked, their sins may grow till they are great. "Let them alone," says God. "In the day of harvest, I will say to the reapers, 'Gather them into bundles, and burn them.'" So, you see, it is God's love to His children, His anxious desire that they may not perish, which often brings them into chastisement on account of sin which, otherwise, they might have escaped. If, then, we are often chastened and sorely vexed. If we are God's children, let us see the loving reason for it and conclude that "we are chastened of the Lord, that we should not be condemned with the world."

II. And now, having explained the Lord's chastisement of His people, I shall occupy but a very few minutes in showing that GOD, BY THUS CHASTENING US, SPARES US FROM BEING CONDEMNED WITH THE WORLD, dwelling simply upon the fact that though the righteous are chastened here, they can never be condemned in the next world.

We are often charged with preaching immoral Doctrine when we say that the righteous man can never be condemned—that he that believes in Christ can never be punished on account of his sins.

Whatever charge may be brought against us, we are not ashamed to repeat our statement, for thus it is written, "There is therefore now no condemnation to them which are in Christ Jesus." The sufferings which God's people feel here are not punishments, but chastisements. If I have ever used the word "punishment" in relation to Believers, it must be understood in its restrictive sense.

God has punished Christ, once and for all, for all the sins which the elect have committed, or ever can commit. And it is not consistent with the justice of God to punish the same offense twice in two different persons. The sufferings of the righteous here are not punitive, they are corrective—they are intended to be chastening. It is not the sword of the judge, it is the rod of the father, which falls upon the Believer. The father may sometimes give his child a sterner and more severe punishment for an offense than even a judge might award. A judge might dismiss a child with a censure for some fault, but the father, when he gets him home, will see him well whipped for it and so, full often, the chastisement of God, in this world, may even seem to be heavier than if it were punitive! Yet we may always remember this for our comfort—that God is not condemning us with the world. When He is smiting us, He is not using the rod with which He will break in pieces the wicked! He is not terrifying us with the awful thunders which shall one day make all Hell quake with fright! He is but putting on an expression of anger that He may cleanse our hearts—and is but using the rod with the hand of love, that He may purge us of that folly which is bound up in the heart of His people.

I have said that a Christian shall never, in the world to come, be condemned for his sin, and it is assuredly true, for the first reason, that God cannot punish twice for one offense. It is also true for the second reason, that God cannot condemn those whom He has justified. That were to reverse what He has once done and so to prove Himself a mutable being! He cannot first give us the witness of forgiveness and afterwards the witness of damnation for guilt. It is not possible for Him to first kiss us with the kiss of His love and then, afterwards, to cast us into Hell. God will not play fast and loose with His children, first justifying them through His Grace and then, afterwards, condemning them through their sin. I say that were to contradict Himself.

God cannot, in the third place, condemn His children because they are His children, and He is their Father. Having taken men into such a relation to Himself as to make Himself their Father, God has in that very act put it beyond His own power to utterly condemn and cast them out. He is Omnipotent—He can do anything as far as His power is concerned—but He cannot belie the instincts of His heart. Now, no father can forget his child—it is not possible—and it is not possible for God, after He has once forgiven and has sealed that forgiveness in the glorious privilege of adoption—it is not possible for Him to answer the cry of, "Abba, Father," with the sentence, "Depart, you cursed!"

And, again, it is impossible for God to condemn those whom He has justified for the reason that if He did so, all His promises and the whole tenor of the Covenant would be violated. It was to save from their sins all those who believe in Him that Jesus died. If, then, these are not saved, every one of them, His death must be in vain. If those whose sins He carried shall be, at last, cast into Hell, then Christ's project of Redemption has never been fully carried out. To suppose a universal Atonement is to suppose that the design of God has been partly frustrated—that Christ has attempted to do something greater than He will really effect. But here is our solid resting place—that the Covenant stands secure and that, in Christ, every stipulation of it is firm—and through Him every single article of it shall be carried out. Now, the complete salvation of all the elect is one part of it and, therefore, chastened though they may be in this world, that is no contradiction to the fact that they shall "not be condemned with the world" hereafter.

I am going to close my discourse with a picture. The Last Great Day is coming. Do you see, yonder, the gathering storm? Do you mark the black clouds as, one after another, they accumulate? For whom is that tempest coming? Can you take a glimpse into the treasure house of God and see His hailstones and coals of fire? Can you discover His lightning, as they are stored up against the Day of Wrath? For whom are these reserved? You shall hear, by-and-by.

Look yonder in another direction, the very opposite. What does that deluge of descending rain mean? What does the rolling of that awful thunder mean? I see, in the center of that storm, a Cross. What do all that terrible display of tempest and of hurricane mean? Why, yonder, there is no sound as yet of storm! It is gathering, but it has not burst. It still gathers but, as yet, not a drop of rain descends. The lightning is bound up in bundles which are not yet loosed. Why is it that, yonder, all is the stillness of a storehouse and a mighty preparation for war, while, over there, that war is going on and all the bolts of God are launched? It means this. God has separated His people from the world. Over yonder His wrath is spending itself, the black clouds are letting out their floods, thunder is poured forth and lightning is flashing—where? Upon the head of the mighty Savior, the dying Jesus!

The wrath must be spent somewhere and so, in all its fury, it is manifesting itself around Christ! And yonder pilgrims who are just caught by a few drops that skirt the terrible tempest, are those for whom that tempest is being endured by their glorious Substitute. Yonder tried and afflicted ones, scared by the lightning and alarmed by the troubling of the tempest—these are the men who have a share in the Substitution of Christ. I say the afflictions of God's people are like the trickling on the skirts of that great tempest—they are the few drops on the margin of the storm which spent itself on Christ. These men, who in this world suffer afflictions—righteously endure them and patiently suffer them for Christ's sake—are those who shall have no storm hereafter—for look, the storm is now gone. All is cleared away and, instead, the sun shines out in its glory above their heads! Angels are descending and on angelic wings they are borne upward to a Temple and to mansions prepared for them in the Presence of their Father.

But look at yonder men and women—they are dancing merrily! Though all overhead is black, not a drop of rain has yet fallen. Mark how they are marrying and giving in marriage, for not a bolt has yet been launched. Who are these? Alas, poor wretches, these are the men for whom the Judge is treasuring up wrath against the Day of Wrath. For them He is reserving fire and brimstone, hot coals of juniper and terrible destruction. They look askance on yonder pilgrims slightly wetted with the storm. They make a mock of yonder poor converted ones, trembling as they hear the rolling thunder. They say, "We hear no tempest! It is all a delusion, there is no storm!" Yes, Sinners, but the day is coming when you shall discover your mistake! You have your portion here, but Believers are happier, as they are all saved for the great hereafter. You have no bands in your death—it is that you may have the tighter bands in Hell! You have few afflictions here—it is that they may be doubled to you hereafter! You go merrily through this world, you carry the lamp of joy with you—it is that your blackness may be the more terrible and your darkness the more awful when you are excluded from earthly joys—and shut up forever in the outer darkness, where there will be weeping, and wailing, and gnashing of teeth!

It is pleasant to pass through a country after a storm has spent itself—to smell the freshness of the herbs after the rain has passed away and to note the drops after they have been turned to diamonds in the sunlight. That is the position of a Christian. He is going through a land where the storm has spent itself, or if there are a few drops, the written page of the Covenant cheers him on and tells him this is not for his destruction. But how terrible is it to witness the approach of a tempest—to see the preparation for the storm, to mark the birds of Heaven as they flutter their wings, to see the cattle as they lay their heads low in terror, to discern the face of the black sky, the sun which shines not and the heavens which give no light! How terrible to stand on the verge of a horrible hurricane—such as occurs, sometimes, in the tropics—to know that we cannot tell how soon the wind may come in fury, tearing up trees from their roots, forcing rocks from their pedestals and hurling down all the dwelling places of man!

And yet, Sinner, this is just your position! There are no hot drops as yet fallen, but a shower of fire is coming. There are no terrible winds blowing on you, but God's tempest shall surely come. As yet, the floods are dammed up by Mercy, but the floodgates shall soon be opened. The bolts of God are yet in His storehouse, but, lo, judgment comes, and how awful shall be that moment when God, robed in vengeance, shall come forth in fury! Where, where, where, O Sinner, will you hide your head, or where will you flee? Oh, that the hand of Mercy may now lead you to Christ! He is freely preached to you, and you know your need of Him! Believe in Him! Cast yourself upon Him and then the fury shall be over and you need not dread to go into eternity, for no storm awaits you there, but quiet, and calm, and rest, and peace forever!

EXPOSITION OF RUTH 1

Verse 1. *Now it came to pass in the days when the judges ruled, that there was a famine in the land. And a certain man of Bethlehem Judah went to sojourn in the country of Moab, he, and his wife, and his two sons.* That was a bad move on their part—better poverty with the people of God, than plenty outside of the covenanted land.

2. *And the name of the man was Elimelech.* "Elimelech?" It means, "my God is King." A man with such a name as that ought not to have left the kingdom where His God was King! But some people are not worthy of the names they bear.

2. *And the name of His wife Naomi, and the name of his two sons Mahlon and Chilion, Ephrathites of Bethlehem Judah. And they came into the country of Moab, and continued there.* That is generally what happens. Those who go into the country of Moab continue there. If Christians go away from their separated life, they are very apt to continue in that condition. It may be easy to say, "I will step aside from the Christian path for just a little while," but it is not so easy to return to it. Usually something or other hampers—the birdlime catches the birds of Paradise and holds them fast.

3, 4. *And Elimelech, Naomi's husband died, and she was left, and her two sons. And they took them wives of the women of Moab; the name of the one was Orpah, and the name of the other Ruth: and they dwelled there about ten years.* Which was about ten years too long! Probably they did not intend to remain so long when they went there. They only meant to be in Moab for a little while, just as Christian people, when they fall into worldly conformity, only purpose to do it once, "for the sake of the girls, to bring them out a little." But it happens to them as it is written here—"and they dwelled there about ten years."

5. *And Mahlon and Chilion died also, both of them; and the woman was left of her two sons and her husband.* That seemed to be her great grief—that she was left. She would have been content to go with them, but she was left to mourn their loss.

6. *Then she arose with her daughters-in-law, that she might return from the country of Moab.* It is often the case that when our idols are broken, we turn back to our God. It is frequently the case that the loss of earthly good leads us to return to our first Husband, for we feel that then it was better with us than it is now. Naomi had also another inducement to return.

6. *For she had heard in the country of Moab how that the LORD had visited His people in giving them bread.* Have any of you professors gone a long way off from God? I wish you knew what plenty there is in the Great Father's house and what a blessed feast there is for these who live with Him! There is no famine in that land! There is plenty of gladness, plenty of comfort, plenty of everything that is joyful to be found there. You need not go to Moab and to her false gods to find pleasure and satisfaction.

7-9. *Therefore she went forth out of the place where she was, and her two daughters-in-law with her; and they went on the way to return unto the land of Judah. And Naomi said unto her two daughters-in-law, Go, return each to her mother's house; the Lord deal kindly with you, as you have dealt with the dead, and with me. The LORD grant you that you may find rest, each of you in the house of her husband. Then she kissed them: and they lifted up their voice, and wept.* Separation was painful to them, for they loved their mother-in-law, a most unselfish person who, even though it was a comfort to her to enjoy their company, thought it would be for their good, in a temporal sense, that they should abide in their own country.

10-14. *And they said unto her, Surely we will return with you unto your people. And Naomi said, Turn again, my daughters: why will you go with me? Are there yet any more sons in my womb, that they may be your husbands? Turn again, my daughters, go your way; for I am too old to have an husband. If I should say, I* have hope, *if I should have an husband also tonight, and should also bear sons; would you tarry for them till they were grown? Would you stay for them from having husbands? No, my daughters; for it grieves me much for your sakes that the hand of the Lord is gone out against me. And they lifted up their voice, and wept again: and Orpah kissed her mother-in-law; but Ruth cleaved unto her.* What a difference there often is between two persons who are under religious impressions at the same time! The one would like to follow Jesus, but the price is too much to pay, so there is a kiss somewhat like that of Judas, and Orpah goes back to her people, and to her idols. But how different was the other case! Ruth was, as it were, glued to Naomi! She "cleaved unto her." Stuck to her and could not be made to go back with her sister.

15-17. *And she said, Behold, your sister-in-law is gone back unto her people, and unto her gods: return you after your sister-in-law. And Ruth said, Entreat me not to leave you, or to return from following after you: for where you go, I will go; and where you lodge, I will lodge: your people shall be my people, and your God my God: where you die, I will die, and there I will be buried: the* LORD *do so to me, and more, also, if anything but death parts you and me.* That was bravely spoken and she meant it, too.

18. *When she saw that she was steadfastly minded to go with her, then she left off speaking unto her.* That is a striking expression, "When she saw that she was steadfastly minded to go with her." O you dear young friends who want to be Christians, how glad we are when we see that you are steadfastly minded to go with the people of God! There are so many who are quickly hot and quickly cold—soon excited towards good things and almost as speedily their ardor cools and they go back into the world. Do ask the Lord to make you steadfastly minded! This is one of the best frames of mind for any of us to be in.

19. *So they two went until they came to Bethlehem. And it came to pass, when they were come to Bethlehem, that all the city was moved about them, and they said, Is this Naomi?* They seemed all to turn out of doors to have a look at these two strangers and especially at Naomi, for she was so different from what she had been when she went away. "And they said, Is this Naomi? Some said, "Is this Naomi?" questioning. Others said it with surprise as a thing incredible, "This Naomi! How can she be the same

woman?" It was very rude of them to turn out, just like people without sympathy do on Ramsgate Pier, to see the sick passengers land. Nobody seems to have said, "Come into our house to lodge," but all questioned, "Is this Naomi?"

20. *And she said unto them, Call me not Naomi.* "Call me not 'pleasant.'"

20. *Call me Mara.* That is, "bitter."

20. *For the Almighty has dealt very bitterly with me.* It was a pity for Naomi to say that, yet I fear that many of us have done the same. We have not borne such sweet testimony to the Lord as we might have done, but have sorrowfully moaned, as this poor woman did.

21. *I went out full.* Why, then, did you go out?

21. *And the LORD has brought me home again empty.* Ah, but He has brought you home again! Oh, if she would but have noticed the mercy there was in it all, she might still have spoken like Naomi! But now she speaks like Mara—bitterness. Her husband and her two boys—all her heart's delight—were with her when she went out. And now that they are gone, she says—

21. *Why then call you me Naomi, seeing the LORD has testified against me, and the Almighty has afflicted me?* Yet it is a sweet thing to be able to trace the hand of God in our affliction, for nothing can come from that hand towards one of His children but that which is good and right! If you will think of those hands of which the Lord says, "I have engraved you upon the palms of My hands," you may rest assured that nothing can come from those hands but what Infinite Wisdom directs and Infinite Love has ordained!

22. *So Naomi returned, and Ruth the Moabitess, her daughter-in-law, with her, which returned out of the country of Moab: and they came to Bethlehem in the beginning of barley harvest.* That is, at the time of the Passover. Let us hope that they received a blessing in observing the ordinances of that time and that they were thus helped to get back to the only right and happy state of heart.

2
RUTH DECIDING FOR GOD

"And Ruth said, Entreat me not to leave you, or to return from following after you: for where you go, I will go; and where you lodge, I will lodge: your people shall be my people, and your God my God."

—Ruth 1:16

THIS WAS A VERY BRAVE, outspoken confession of faith. Please notice that it was made by a woman, a young woman, a poor woman, a widow woman and a foreigner. Remembering all that, I should think there is no condition of gentleness, or of obscurity, or of poverty, or of sorrow which should prevent any body from making an open confession of allegiance to God when faith in the Lord Jesus Christ has been exercised. If that is your experience, my dear Friend, then whoever you may be, you will find an opportunity, somewhere or other, of declaring that you are on the Lord's side. I am glad that all candidates for membership in our Church make their confession of faith at our Church Meetings. I have been told that such an ordeal must keep a great many from joining us, yet I notice that where there is no such ordeal, they often have very few members—but here we are with 5,600 or thereabouts, in Church fellowship and, very seldom, if ever, finding anybody kept back by having to make an open confession of faith in Christ. It does the man, the woman, the boy, or the girl—whoever it is—so much good for once, at least, to say right out straight, "I am a Believer in the Lord Jesus Christ and I am not ashamed of it," that I do not think we shall ever deviate from our custom. I have also noticed that when people have once confessed Christ before men, they are very apt to do it again somewhere else. And they thus acquire a kind of boldness and outspokenness upon religious matters—and a holy courage as followers of Christ—which more than make up for any self-denial and trembling which the effort may have cost them.

I think Naomi was quite right to drive Ruth, as it were, to take this brave stand in which it became an absolute necessity for her to speak right straight out and say, in the words of our text, "Entreat me not to leave you, or to return from following after you: for where you go, I will go; and where you lodge, I will lodge: your people shall be my people, and your God my God." What is there for any of us to be ashamed of in acknowledging that we belong to the Lord Jesus Christ? What can there be that should cause us to be ashamed of Jesus, or make us blush to acknowledge His name?—

"ASHAMED OF JESUS?

> That dear Friend,
> On whom my hopes of Heaven depend?
> No, when I blush, be this my shame,
> That I no more revere His name."

We ought to be ashamed of being ashamed of Jesus! We ought to be afraid of being afraid to acknowledge Him! We ought to tremble at trembling to confess Him and to resolve that we will take all suitable opportunities that we can find of saying, first to relatives, and then to all others with whom we come into contact, "We serve the Lord Christ."

I should think that Naomi was—certainly she ought to have been—greatly cheered by hearing this declaration from Ruth, especially the last part of it—"Your people shall be my people, and your God my God." Naomi had suffered great temporal loss. She had lost her husband and her two sons, but now she had found the soul of her daughter-in-law. And I believe that, according to the scales of true judgment, there ought to have been more joy in her heart at the conversion of Ruth's soul than grief over the death of her husband and her sons. Our Lord Jesus has told us that "there is joy in the presence of the angels of God over one sinner that repents." And I always understand, by that expression, that there is joy in the heart of God, Himself, over every sinner's repentance! Well, then, if Naomi's husband and sons were true Believers—if they had been walking aright before the Lord—as, let us hope, they had done, she need not have felt such sorrow for them as could at all compare with the joy of her daughter-in-law being saved.

Perhaps, some of you, dear Friends, have had bereavements in your homes, but if the death—the temporal death—of one should be the means of the spiritual life of another, there is a clear gain! I am sure there is and though you may have gone weeping to the grave, yet if you have evidence that, with those tears, there were also tears of repentance on the part of others of your family—and with that sad glance into the grave there was also a believing look at the dying, risen, and living Savior—you are decidedly a gainer and you need not say with Naomi, "I went out full, and the Lord has brought me home, again, empty." Really, Naomi, with her converted daughter-in-law at her side, if she had only been able to look into the future, might have been a happier woman than when she went away with her husband and her boys, for now she had with her one who was to be in the direct line of the progenitors of Christ—a right royal woman—for I count that the line of Christ is the true imperial line and that they were the most highly honored among men and women who were in any way associated with the birth of the Savior into this world. And Ruth, though a Moabitess, was one of those who were elected to share in this high privilege. So I beg you, if you have been sorrowful because of any deaths in your family circle, pray God to outweigh that sorrow with a greater measure of joy because, by His Grace, He has brought other members of your family to trust in Jesus!

Another thought strikes me here. That is, that it was when Naomi returned to the land which she ought never to have left—it was when she came out from the idolatrous Moabites among whom she had, as you see, relatives, and friends, and acquaintances—it was when she said, "I will go back to my own country, and people, and God"—that then the Lord gave her the soul of this young woman who was so closely related to her. It may be that some of you professedly Christian people have been living at a distance from God. You have not led the separated life. You have tried to be friendly with the world as well as with Christ—and your children are not growing up as you wish they would. You say that your sons are not turning out well and that your girls are dressy, flighty and worldly. Do you wonder that it is so?

"Oh," you say, "I have gone a good way to try to please them, thinking that, perhaps, by doing so, I might win them for Christ!" Ah, you will never win any soul to the right by a compromise with the wrong! It is decision for Christ and His Truth that has the greatest power in the family and the world, too. If a soldier in the barracks is converted and he says, "I mean to be a Christian, but, at the same time, I will join with the other men as much as I can. I will sometimes step into the tavern with them," and so forth, he will do no good. But the moment he boldly takes his stand for his new Captain and is known to be a Christian—his comrades may begin to scoff at him, but they will also begin to be impressed—and if he bravely maintains that stand and never gives way in the least degree, but is faithful to his Lord and Master, then he will be likely to see conversions among his fellow soldiers.

It was while Naomi was on her way back to her own land that she heard the good news that her dear daughter-in-law had decided to be a follower of Jehovah and to say, "Your people shall be my people, and your God my God." This gave her great joy, but how must some of you Christian people feel when you find out that others have been caused to stumble through your living at a distance from Christ? What pangs of remorse will seize you when you discover that your arm has been paralyzed for good—that you have been unable to lead others to the Savior because you, yourself, were living so far from Him that it was a serious question whether you were not growing to be a worshipper of the Moabite idols and giving up altogether your profession of being a follower of the one true God?

Now, with this as a preface, I come directly to the subject of the text. Here is a young woman who says to a follower of Jehovah, "Your people shall be my people, and your God my God."

I. My first observation is that AFFECTION FOR THE GODLY SHOULD INFLUENCE US TO GODLINESS.

It did so in this case. Affection for their godly mother-in-law influenced both Orpah and Ruth for a time "and they said unto her, Surely we will return with you unto your people." They were both drawn part of the way towards Canaan, but, alas, natural affection has not sufficient power, in itself, to draw anybody to a decision for God! It may be helpful to that end. It may be one of the "cords of a man" and "bands of love" which God, in His infinite mercy, often uses in drawing sinners to Himself, but there has to be something more than that mere human affection. Still, it ought to be of some service in leading to a decision and it is a very dreadful thing when those who have godly parents seem to be the worse, rather than the better for that fact, or when men, who have Christian wives, rebel against the Light of God and become all the more wicked because God has blessed their homes with godly women who speak to them lovingly and tenderly concerning the claims of the religion of Jesus. That is a terrible state of affairs, for it ought always to be the case that our affection for godly people should help to draw us towards godliness. In Ruth's case, by the grace of God, it was the means of leading her to the decision expressed in our text, "Your people shall be my people, and your God my God."

Many forces may be combined to bring others to this decision. First, there is the influence of companionship. Nobody doubts that evil company tends to make a man bad. And it is equally sure that good companionship has a tendency to influence men towards that which is good. It is a happy thing to have side by side with you one whose heart is full of love to God. It is a great blessing to have as a mother a true saint, or to have as a brother or a sister one who fears the Lord. And it is a special privilege to be linked for life, in the closest bonds, with one whose prayers may rise with ours, and whose praises may also mingle with ours. There is something about Christian companionship which must count in the right direction unless the heart is resolutely bent on mischief.

There is something more than this, however, and that is the influence of admiration. There can be no doubt whatever that Ruth looked with loving reverence and admiration upon Naomi, for she saw in her a character which won her heart's esteem and affection. The few glimpses which we have of that godly woman, in this Book of Ruth, show us that she was a most disinterested and unselfish person—not one who, because of her own great sorrow, would burden others with it and pull them down to her own level in order that they might in some way assist her. She was one who considered the interests of others rather than her own—and all such persons are sure to win admiration and esteem. When a Christian man so lives that others see something about him which they do not perceive in themselves, that is one way in which they are often attracted towards the Christian life. When the sick Christian is patient. When the poor Christian is cheerful. When the Believer in Christ is forgiving, generous, tenderhearted, sympathetic, honest and upright, then it is that observers say, "Here is something worth looking into—from where comes all this excellence?" And they take knowledge of them that they have been with Jesus and that they have learned these things of Him—and in that way they are, themselves, inclined to become His followers.

Nor is it only by companionship and admiration that people are won to the Savior. There is also the influence of instruction. I have no doubt that Naomi gave her daughter-in-law much helpful teaching. Ruth would want to know about Naomi's God and Naomi would be only too glad to tell her all she knew. When the Spaniards went over to South America, they treated the poor natives so badly that the Indians did not wish to know anything about the Spaniards' god, for they thought, from the cruelties they had suffered, that he must be a devil! And there are certain sorts of professors who are so unkind—they have such an absence of everything gentle and generous about them—that one does not want to know anything about their god, for if they are like he, he probably is the devil!

But, dear Friends, it ought not to be so with us. We should make people want to know what our religion really is and then be ready to tell them! I have no doubt that, many a time, in the land of Moab, when her daughters-in-law ran in to see her, Naomi would begin telling them about the deliverance at the Red Sea and how the Lord brought His people through the wilderness and how the goodly land, which flowed with milk and honey, had been given to them by the hand of Joshua. Then she would tell them about the tabernacle and its worship, and talk to them about the lamb, and the red heifer, and the bullock, and the sin-offering and so on. And it was thus, probably, that Ruth's heart had been won to Jehovah, the God of Israel. And, perhaps, for that reason—because of Naomi's instruction—Ruth said to her, "'Your people shall be my people.' I know so much about them that I want to be numbered with them. 'And your God shall be my God.' You have told me about Him—what wonders He has worked—and I have resolved to trust myself under the shadow of His wings." Well, Beloved, it ought to be thus with us, also. We should take care that the influence of our companionship, the influence of our lives in which there should be something for observers to admire and the influence of our conversation, which should be full of gracious instruction, should lead those who come under our influence in the right way.

Besides that, I have no doubt that some persons are drawn towards good things by a desire to cheer the godly persons whom they love. And though I do not put this forward as one of the highest and strongest motives, yet I do feel at liberty to suggest to some young people here that their sins are a great grief to their loving fathers and mothers and that, if their hearts were given to Christ, it would fill the whole house with holy joy! It was a great joy to me when my sons were born, but it was an infinitely surpassing joy as, one after the other, they told me that they had sought and found the Savior! To pray with them, to point them yet more fully to Christ, to hear the story of their spiritual troubles and to help them out of their spiritual difficulties was an intense satisfaction to my soul. Ah, my young Friends, you do not know how much those who love you would be cheered if you were converted—especially any of you who have not lived as you should have done—who have, perhaps, even gone away from home and acted in a way that might well bring your father's gray hairs in sorrow to the grave. I think that he would almost dance with delight if he could only hear that you were truly converted to God!

I know a minister who took out of his pocket an old letter that was nearly worn to pieces. He made a journey from the country to bring it up for me to see. It was not really old—it was worn out because he had so constantly taken it out to read. It was somewhat to this effect. His son had been such a scapegrace and such a disgrace to his family that he was helped to go abroad—and he came to London to join the ship. As he had heard his father speak of me, he thought that he would spend his last Thursday night, before starting on the Friday morning, in hearing me in this Tabernacle. And here God met with him, for I was moved by the Holy Spirit to say, "Here you are, Jack—going away from home, from your father's house, oh, that the great Father in Heaven would take you to Himself!" It happened that his name was Jack, so it was the very words for him—and the Lord blessed it to him then and there. He went to America. He did not write to his father to tell him about his conversion till he had had time to prove the reality of it. But when he had been baptized and had joined the Church, and walked consistently for six months, he sent the good news home. The old man said, "I thought he might have been lost at sea, but the Lord had saved him through your preaching. God bless you, Sir!" I had a thousand blessings heaped upon my head by that grateful father. It was only a simple sermon that I had preached on a Thursday night, but it was the means of that son's conversion and it was the source of great joy to that father—he did not mind about his son being in America, or what he was doing—so long as he had become a true Believer in the Lord Jesus Christ! What a mercy it would be if this sermon should be blessed as that one was!

I think, too, that there was another thing which had great influence over Ruth, as it has had over a great many other people. That is, the fear of separation. "Ah," said one to me only last week, "it used to trouble me greatly when my wife went downstairs to the communion and I had to go home, or to remain with the spectators in the gallery. I did not like to be separated from her even here. And then, Sir, the thought stole over me, 'What if I have to be divided from her forever and ever?'" I think that a similar reflection ought, with the blessing of God, to impress a good many. Young man, if you live and die impenitent, you will see your mother no more, except from an awful distance, with a great gulf fixed between her and you, so that she cannot cross over to you, or you go over to her! There will come a day when one shall be taken and another left. And before the great separation takes place at the Judgment Seat of Christ—when there shall be a division made between the goats and the sheep, and between the tares and the wheat—I implore you to let the influence of the godly whom you love help to draw you towards decision for God and His Christ.

II. My time would fail me if I dwelt longer on this point, though it is a very interesting one, so I must pass on to my second observation which is, that which RESOLVES TO GODLINESS WILL BE TESTED. Ruth speaks very positively—"Your people shall be my people, and your God my God." This was her resolve, but it was a resolve which had already been put to the test and she had, in great measure, satisfactorily passed through it.

First, it had been tested by the poverty and the sorrow of her mother-in-law. Naomi said, "The Almighty has dealt very bitterly with me," yet Ruth says, "Your God shall be my God." I like that brave resolution of the young Moabitess. Some people say, "We would like to be converted, for we want to be happy." Yes, but suppose you knew that you would not be happy after conversion? You still ought to wish to have this God to be your God. Naomi has lost her husband, she has lost her sons, she has lost everything—she is going back penniless to Bethlehem—and yet her daughter-in-law says to her, "Your God shall be my God." Oh, dear Friends, if you can share the lot of Christians when they are in trouble. If you can take God and affliction. If you can accept Christ and a cross—then your decision to be His follower is true and real! It has been tested by the afflictions and the trials which you know belong to the people of God, yet you are content to suffer with them in taking their God to be your God, too.

Next, Ruth's decision had been tested when she was bidden to count the cost Naomi had put the whole case before her. She had told her daughter-in-law that there was no hope that she should ever bear a son who could become a husband to Ruth—and that she had better stay and find a husband in her own land. She set before her the dark side of the case—possibly too earnestly. She seemed as if she wanted to persuade her to go back, though I do not think that, in her heart, she could really have wished her to do so. But, my young Friend, before you say to any Christian, "Your people shall be my people, and your God my God," count the cost! Remember if you are following an evil trade, you will have to give it up. If you have formed bad habits, you will have to forsake them. And if you have had bad companions, you will have to leave them. There are a great many things which have afforded you pleasure which must become painful to you and must be renounced. Are you prepared to follow Christ through the mire and the slough, as well as along the high road and down in the valley as well as up upon the hills? Are you ready to carry His Cross as you hope, afterwards, to share His crown? If you can stand the test in detail—such a test as Christ set before those who wanted to be His followers on earth—then is your decision a right one!

Ruth had been tried, too, by the apparent coldness of one in whom she trusted and whom she had a right to trust, for Naomi did not at all encourage her. Indeed, she seemed to discourage her. I am not sure that Naomi is to be blamed for that and I am not certain that she is to be much praised. You know, it is quite possible for you to encourage people too much. I have known some encouraged in their doubts and fears till they never could get out of them. At the same time, you can certainly very easily chill enquirers and seekers. And though Naomi showed her love to Ruth, yet she did not seem to have any very great desire to bring her to follow Jehovah. This is a test that many young people find to be very trying—but this young woman said to her mother-in-law, "Entreat me not to leave you, or to return from following after you: for where you go, I will go; and where you lodge, I will lodge: your people shall be my people, and your God my God."

Another trial for Ruth was the drawing back of her sister-in-law. Orpah kissed Naomi and left her. And you know the influence of one young person upon another when they are of the same age, or when they are related as these two were. You went to the revival meeting with a friend and she was as much impressed as you were. She has gone back to the world and the temptation is for you to do the same. Can you stand out against it? You two young men went to hear the same preacher and you both felt the force of the Word of God, but your companion has gone back to where he used to be. Can you hold out, now, and say, "I will follow Christ alone if I cannot find a companion to go with me?" If so, it is well with you—

> "Can you cleave to your Lord? Can you cleave to your Lord,
> When the many turn aside?
> Can you witness He has the living Word,
> And none upon earth beside?
> And can you endure with the virgin band,
> The lowly and pure in heart,
> Who, wherever the Lamb does lead,
> From His footsteps never depart?
> Do you answer, 'We can'? Do you answer, 'We can,
> Through His love's constraining power'?
> But, ah, remember the flesh is weak,
> And will shrink in the trial-hour.
> Yet yield to His love, who round you now,
> The bands of a man would cast
> The cords of His love, who was given for you,
> To the altar binding you fast."

But one of the worst trials that Ruth had was the silence of Naomi I think that is what is meant, for after she had solemnly declared that she would follow the Lord, we read, "When she saw that she was steadfastly minded to go with her, then she stopped speaking unto her." She left off stating the black side of the case, but she does not appear to have talked to her about the bright side. "She stopped speaking unto her." The good woman was so sorrowful that she could not talk! Her heart-break was so great that she could not converse. And such silence must have been very trying to Ruth—and when a young person has just joined the people of God, it is a severe test to be brought face to face with a very mournful Christian and not to get one encouraging word!

Sometimes, Brothers and Sisters, we must swallow our own bitter pills as fast as we can, that we may not discourage others by making a wry face over them. It is sometimes the very best thing a sorrowful person can do to say, "I must not be sad. Here is young So-and-So coming in. I must be cheerful, for here comes one who might be discouraged by my grief." You remember how the Psalmist, when he was in a very mournful state of mind, said, "If I say, I will speak thus—behold, I should offend against the generation of your children. When I thought to know this, it was too painful for me"? Let it be too painful for us to give any cause for stumbling or disquietude to those who have just come to the Savior, but let us cheer and encourage them all we can. Still, Naomi's silence did not discourage Ruth—she was evidently a strong-minded, though gentle young woman, and she gave herself up to God and His people without any reserve. Even though she might not be helped much by the older Believer and might even be discouraged by her—and still more by the departure of her sister-in-law, Orpah—yet she still pressed on in the course she had chosen!

Well, you do the same, Mary. And you, Jane, and John, and Thomas. Will you be like Mr. Pliable and go back to the City of Destruction? Or will you, like Christian, pursue your way and steadfastly hold on through the Slough of Despond, or whatever else may be in your pathway to the Celestial City?

III. Now, thirdly, and very briefly, TRUE GODLINESS MUST MAINLY LIE IN THE CHOICE OF GOD. That is the very pith of the text—"Your God shall be my God."

First, dear Friends, God is the Believer's choicest possession. Indeed, it is the distinguishing mark of a Christian that he acknowledges a God. Naomi had not much else—no husband, no son, no lands, no gold, no silver, no pleasure, even—but she had a God. Come, now, my Friend, are you determined that, henceforth and forever, the Lord shall be your chief possession? Can you say, "God shall be mine; my faith shall grasp Him, now, and hold Him fast?" Next, God was, henceforth, to Ruth, as He had been to Naomi—her Ruler and Law-Giver. When anyone truthfully says, "God shall be my God," there is some practical meaning about that declaration. It means, "He shall influence me. He shall direct me. He shall lead me. He shall govern me. He shall be my King. I will yield to Him and obey Him in everything. I will endeavor to do all things according to His will. God shall be my God." You must not want to take God to be your helper, in the sense of making Him to be your servant, but to be your Master and so to help you. Dear friends, does the Holy Spirit lead you to make this blessed choice and to declare, "This God shall be mine, my Law-Giver and Ruler from this time forth?"

Well, then, He must also be your Instructor. At the present day, I am afraid that nine people out of ten do not believe in the God who is revealed to us in the Bible. "What?" you say. It is so, I grieve to say it. I can point you to newspapers, to magazines, to periodicals and also to pulpits by the score in which there is a new god set up to be worshipped—not the God of the Old Testament—He is said to be too strict, too severe, too stern for our modern teachers. They do not believe in Him. The God of Abraham is dethroned by many, nowadays, and in His place they have a spineless god, like those of whom Moses spoke, "new gods that came newly up, whom your fathers feared not." They shudder at the very mention of the God of the Puritans! If Jonathan Edwards were to rise from the dead, they would not listen to him for a minute—they would say that they had quite a new god since his day—but, Brothers and Sisters, I believe in the God of Abraham, and of Isaac, and of Jacob! This God is my God—yes, the God that drowned Pharaoh and his host at the Red Sea and moved His people to sing "Hallelujah" as He did it! The God that caused the earth to open and swallow up Korah, Dathan and Abiram and all their company—a terrible God is the God whom I adore—He is the God and Father of our Lord and Savior Jesus Christ, full of mercy, compassion and Grace, tender and gentle, yet just and dreadful in His holiness and terrible out of His holy places. This is the God whom we worship and he who comes to Him in Christ, and trusts in Him, will take Him to be his Instructor—and so shall he learn aright all that he needs to know. But woe unto the men of this day who have made unto themselves a calf of their own devising which has no power to bless or to save them! "Your God" says Ruth to Naomi—not another god—not Chemosh or Moloch, but Jehovah—"shall be my God." And so she took Him to be her Instructor, as we, also, must do.

Then, let us take Him to be our entire trust and stay. O my beloved Friends, the happiest thing in life is to trust God—first to trust Him with your soul through Jesus Christ the Savior—and then to trust Him with everything and in everything. I am speaking what I know! The life of sense is death, but the life of faith is life, indeed! Trust God about temporary things—no, I do not know any division between temporary things and spiritual things—trust God about everything! About your daily livelihood, about your health, about your wife, about your children—live a life of faith in God and you will truly live and all things will be right about you. It is because we get to partly trusting God and partly trusting ourselves that we are often so unhappy. But when, by simple faith, you just cast yourselves on God, then you find the highest joy and bliss that is possible on earth—and a whole series of wonders is spread out before you! Your life becomes like a miracle, or a succession of miracles, God hearing your prayers and answering you out of Heaven, delivering you in the time of trial, supplying your every need and leading you always onward by a matchless way which you know not, which every moment shall cause you greater astonishment and delight as you see the unfolding of the Character of God. Oh, that each one of you would say, "This God shall be my God. I will trust Him. By His Grace I will trust Him now."

IV. The last thing is that THIS DECISION SHOULD LEAD US TO CAST IN OUR LOT WITH GOD'S PEOPLE AS WELL AS WITH HIMSELF, for Ruth said, "Your people shall be my people."

She might have said, "You are not well spoken of, you Jews, you Israelites. The Moabites, among whom I have lived, hate you." But, in effect, she said, "I am no Moabitess now. I am going to belong to Israel and to be spoken against, too. They have all manner of bad things to say in Moab about Bethlehem-Judah, but I do not mind that, for I am going to be, from now on, an inhabitant of Bethlehem and to be reckoned in the number of the Bethlehem people, for no longer am I of Moab and the Moabites."

Now, dear Friend, will you thus cast in your lot with God's people and, though they are spoken against, will you be willing to be spoken against, too? I daresay that the Bethlehem people were not all that Ruth could have wished them to be. Even Naomi was not—she was too sad and sorrowful—but, still, I expect that Ruth thought that her mother-in-law was a better woman than she was herself. I have heard people find fault with the members of our Churches and say that they cannot join with them for they are such an inferior sort of people. Well, I know a great many different sorts of people and, after all, I shall be quite content to be numbered with God's people, as I see them even in His visible Church, rather than to be numbered with any other persons in the whole world! I count the despised people of God the best company I have ever met with—and I often say of this Tabernacle, as I hope members of other Churches can say of their own places of worship—

> "Here my best friends, my kindred dwell, Here God, my Savior, reigns."

"Oh!" says one, "I will join the church when I can find a perfect one." Then you will never join any. "Ah," you say, "but perhaps I may." Well, but it will not be a perfect church the moment you have joined it, for it will cease to be perfect as soon as it receives you into its membership! I think that if a Church is such as Christ can love, it is such as I can love. And if it is such that Christ counts it as his Church, I may well be thankful to be a member of it. Christ "loved the Church and gave Himself for it"—then may I not think it an honor to be allowed to give myself to it?

Ruth was not joining a people out of whom she expected to get much. Shame on those who think to join the church for what they can get! Yet the loaves and fishes are always a bait for some people. But there was Ruth, going with Naomi to Bethlehem—and all that the townsfolk would do would be to turn out and stare at them and say, "Is this Naomi? And pray who is this young woman that has come with her? This Naomi—dear me! How altered she is! How worn she looks! Quite the old woman to what she was when she left us." Not much sympathy was given to them, as far as I gather from that remark, yet Ruth seemed to say, "I do not care how they treat me. They are God's people, even if they have a great many faults and imperfections, and I am going to join them."

And I invite all of you who can say to us, "Your God is our God," to join with the people of God, openly, visibly, manifestly, decidedly, without any hesitancy, even though you may gain nothing by it! Perhaps you will not, but, on the other hand, you will bring a good deal to it, for that is the true spirit of Christ. "It is more blessed to give than to receive." Yet, in any case, cast in your lot with the people of God and share and share alike with them.

I conclude by saying that whatever the other Bethlehem people might be, there was among them one notable being, and it was worthwhile to join the nation for the sake of union with him. Ruth found it all out by degrees. There was a near kinsman among those people and his name was Boaz. She went to glean in his field and, by-and-by, she was married to him. Ah, that was the reason why I cast in my lot with the people of God, for I said to myself, "There is One among them who, whatever faults they may have, is so fair and lovely that He more than makes up for all their imperfections! My Lord Jesus Christ, in the midst of His people, makes them all fair in His fairness and makes me feel that to be poor with the poorest and most illiterate of the Church of Christ, meeting in a village barn, is an unspeakable honor since He is among them!"

Our Lord Jesus Christ Himself is always present wherever two or three are gathered together in His name. If His name is on the list, there may be a number of odds and ends put down with Him—members of different denominations, some strange persons, some very old people—as long as His name is on the list, I do not mind about what others are

there, put my name down! Oh, that I might have the eternal honor of having my name written even at the bottom of the page beneath the name of Jesus, my Lord, the Lamb! As Boaz was there, it was enough for Ruth, and as Christ is here, that is quite enough for me! So I hope I have said sufficient to persuade you, who say that our God is your God, to come and join with us, or with some other part of Christ's Church and so to make His people to be your people. And mind you, do it at once, and in the Scriptural fashion, and God bless you in the doing of it, for Christ's sake! Amen.

3
RUTH'S REWARD—OR, CHEER FOR CONVERTS

"The Lord recompense your work, and a full reward be given you of the Lord God of Israel under whose wings you are come to trust."

—Ruth 2:12

THIS WAS THE LANGUAGE OF Boaz, a man of substance and of note in Bethlehem, to a poor stranger of whom he had heard that she had left her kindred and the idols of her nation, that she might become a worshipper of the living and true God. He acted a noble part when he cheered her and bade her be of good courage, now that she was casting in her lot with Naomi and the chosen nation. Observe that he saluted her with words of tender encouragement, for this is precisely what I want all the elder Christians among you to do to those who are the counterparts of Ruth. You who have long been Believers in the Lord Jesus, who have grown rich in experience, who know the love and faithfulness of our Covenant God and who are strong in the Lord and in the power of His might, I want you to make a point of looking out for the young converts and speaking goodly and comfortable words to them, whereby they may be cheered and strengthened. There is a text, a very short one, which I would like to often preach from in reference to those who are newly saved, and I would invite you to be continually practicing it. That text is, "Encourage him." So many throw cold water upon the aspirants after holiness that I would urge others of you to heartily cheer them. Where spiritual life is weak, it should be nurtured with affectionate care. We desire to cherish, not to censure. That the lambs may grow, they must be shepherded. That the tender babes in the household may become strong members of the Divine family, they must be nursed and fed. If Ruth is to be happy in the land of Israel, a Boaz must look after her and be her true friend. Let her nearest kinsmen be speedy in fulfilling this duty.

I have no doubt that much sorrow might be prevented if words of encouragement were more frequently spoken fitly and in season and, therefore, to withhold them is sin. I am afraid that many poor souls have remained in darkness, shut in within themselves, when two or three minutes' brotherly cheer might have taken down the shutters and let in the light of day. Many matters are real difficulties to young Believers, which are not difficulties to us who have been longer in the Way. You and I could clear up, in ten minutes' conversation, questions and doubts which cause our uninstructed friends months of misery. Why are we so reticent when a word would send our weaker Brothers and Sisters on their way rejoicing? Therefore I entreat all of you, whom God has greatly blessed, to look after those that are of low estate in spiritual things—try to cheer and encourage them. As you do this, God will bless you in return, but, if you neglect this tender duty, it may be that you, yourselves, will grow despondent and be in need of friendly succor. Encouragement is due to young converts—every Ruth ought to be comforted when she casts in her lot with the people of God.

I think I can say for every Christian here that the young converts among us have our very best wishes. We desire for them every good and spiritual gift. It will be our wisdom to turn our kindly wishes into prayers. Wishes are lame, but prayer has legs, yes, wings, with which it runs and even flies, towards God! Wishes are baskets, but prayer fills them with bread! Wishes are clouds, but prayer is the rain! Look how Boaz, wishing well, as he did to the humble maiden from Moab, spoke with her and then spoke with God in prayer for her. I take it that my text is a prayer as well as a benediction—"Jehovah recompense your work, and a full reward be given you of Jehovah, God of Israel, under whose wings you are come to trust." Let us pray more than ever for the feeble-minded and the young! Think of them whenever the King grants you an audience. Search them out with kindly care, as a shepherd looks for his young lambs—and then lay them in the bosom of your love and carry them over rough places.

We would, in all probability, see a much more rapid growth in Grace among our young converts if they were better nursed and watched over. Some of us owed much to old, experienced Christians in our younger days. I know I did. I shall forever respect the memory of a humble servant in the school where I was usher, at New Market—an old woman who talked with me concerning the things of the Kingdom and taught me the way of the Lord more perfectly. She knew the Doctrines of Grace better than many a doctor of divinity and she held them with the tenacious grasp of one who found her life in them. It was my great privilege to help her in her old age and but a little while ago she passed away to Heaven. Many things did I learn of her which, today, I delight to preach! Let it be said of us, when we, too, grow old, that those who were children when we were young were helped by us to become useful in their riper years. They will not forget us if we have been to them what Aquila and Priscilla were to Apollos, or Ananias to Paul, or Paul to Timothy. They will pray for us and God will bless us in answer to their prayers when the grasshopper becomes a burden to us and our infirmities are multiplied.

Having thus introduced the text, let us notice in this model word of encouragement, what the convert has done that we should encourage him. Secondly, what that full reward is which he will receive. And, thirdly, following out the historical connection of the text, I should like to conclude by noticing what figure sets forth this full reward—a reward which we desire for every Ruth who has left those who were outside of the Covenant in Moab to come and join herself with the Israel of God—and the God of Israel.

I. First, then, WHAT HAS THE YOUNG CONVERT DONE? We illustrate the subject by the instance of Ruth. Many young converts deserve encouragement because they have left all their old associates.

Ruth, no doubt, had many friends in her native country, but she tore herself away to cling to Naomi and Naomi's God. Perhaps she parted from a mother and a father—if they were alive, she certainly left them to go to the Israelites' country. Possibly she bade adieu to brothers and sisters, certainly she left old friends and neighbors, for she resolved to go with Naomi and share her lot. She said, "Entreat me not to leave you, or to return from following after you: for where you go, I will go, and where you lodge, I will lodge. Your people shall be my people, and your God my God. Where you die, will I die and there will I be buried. The Lord do so to me and more, also, if anything but death parts you and me."

The young convert is an emigrant from the world and has become, for Christ's sake, an alien. Possibly he had many companions—friends who made him merry, after their fashion—men of fascinating manners who could easily provoke his laughter and make the hours dance by. But, because he found in them no savor of Christ, he has forsaken them and for Christ's sake, they have forsaken him. Among his old associates he has become as a speckled bird and they are all against him. You may, perhaps, have seen a canary which has flown from its home, where it enjoyed the fondness of its mistress—you may have seen it out among the sparrows. They pursue it as though they would tear it to pieces and they give it no rest anywhere. Just so the young convert—being no longer of the same feather as his comrades—is the subject of their persecution. He endures trials of cruel mockings and these are as hot irons to the soul. He is now, to them, a hypocrite and a fanatic—they honor him with ridiculous names by which they express their scorn. In their hearts they crown him with a fool's cap and write him down as both idiot and stupid. He will need to exhibit years of holy living before they will be forced into respect for him—and all this because he is quitting their Moab to join with Israel!

Why should he leave them? Has he grown better than they? Does he pretend to be a saint? Can he not drink with them as he once did? He is a protest against their excesses and men don't care for such protests. Can he not sing a jolly song as they do? Indeed, he has turned saint, and what is a saint but a hypocrite? He is a bit too precise and Puritanical and is not to be endured in their free society! According to the grade in life, this opposition takes one form or another, but in no case does Moab admire the Ruth who deserts her idols to worship the God of Israel.

It is not natural that the Prince of Darkness should care to lose his subjects, or that the men of the world should love those who shame them. Is it not most meet that you older Christian people, who have long been separated from the world and are hardened against its jeers, should step in and defend the newcomers? Should you not say, "Come with us and we will do you good—we will be better friends to you than those you have left. We will accompany you on a better road than that from which you have turned and we will find you better joys than worldlings can ever know"? When our great King is represented as saying to His spouse, "Forget, also, your own people and your father's house," He adds, "so shall the King greatly desire your beauty, for He is your Lord." Thus He gives her new company to supply the place of that which she gives up.

Let us gather a hint from this and make a society for those whom the world casts out. Perhaps there has come into this house, at this time, a man or woman who has just rushed out of the City of Destruction, only too glad to be outside its walls. The poor soul does not know which way to run, only he knows that he must run away from his former evil place, for he finds that the city is to be destroyed. O Brothers and Sisters, while such fugitives are wondering which way to go and their evil companions are inviting them to return, step in and show them the true place of shelter! Run with them to the clefts of the Rock. Lift them up if they stumble! Guide them if they miss their way. Fend off their former tempters—form a bodyguard around them—escort them till they are out of immediate danger! Charm them with your loving conversation till they forget their false friends. When Ruth had left her former connections, it was wise and kind for Boaz to address her in the words of comfort which I will again quote to you—"The Lord recompense your work, and a full reward be given you of the Lord God of Israel, under whose wings you are come to trust."

Next, Ruth, having left her old companions, had come among strangers. She was not yet at home in the land of Israel, but confessed herself, "a stranger." She knew Naomi, but in the whole town of Bethlehem she knew no one else. When she came into the harvest field, the neighbors were gleaning, but they were no neighbors of hers—no glance of sympathy fell upon her from them—perhaps they looked at her with cold curiosity. They may have thought, "What business has this Moabitess to come here to take away a part of the gleaning which belongs to the poor of Israel?" I know that such feelings do arise among country people when a stranger from another parish comes gleaning in the field. Ruth was a foreigner and, of course, in their eyes, an intruder. She felt herself to be alone, though under the wings of Israel's God.

Boaz very properly felt that she should not think that courtesy and kindness had died out in Israel and he made a point, though he was by far her superior in station, to go to her and speak a word of encouragement to her. Should not certain of you follow the same practice? May I not call you to do so at once? There will come into our assemblies those that have been lately impressed with a sense of their guilt, or have newly sought and found the Savior—should they be suffered to remain strangers among us? Should not recognition, companionship and hospitality be extended to them to make them feel at home with us? I would sincerely assure any that have come to this Tabernacle for a time and are still unnoticed, that they are singularly unfortunate, for, as a rule, a stranger is looked after and, in every case, he will be welcomed.

If you have been overlooked, you must have been sitting in rather an odd part of the building, for certain of our friends give themselves to the work of hunting up newcomers and conversing with them—so much so that now and then I get complaints of their supposed intrusion! Those complaints much delight me, for they show that earnestness still survives among us! Be prudent, gentle and courteous, of course, but do be on the watch for any who are seeking the Lord and are desirous to unite with His people! I have occasionally to hear a friend say, "Sir, I attended your ministry for months, but those who sat with me in the pew never took the slightest notice of me. I often wished they would, for I was really desirous to be led by the hand to the Savior."

I do not like to hear that accusation! I would infinitely rather that people should complain that you spoke too much of religion to them than that you never said a word! Your supposed intrusion might be greatly to your credit, but your silent indifference must be to your dishonor. Let us try, with all our hearts, to look upon every man that no single seeking soul shall feel itself deserted. Seekers should be spared the agony of crying, "No man cares for my soul!" Are you a Believer? Then you are my Brother. We are no more strangers and foreigners, but fellow citizens with the saints and of the household of God! We would lay ourselves out to bring our fellow men to Jesus and to aid new converts in finding perfect peace at His feet. Let us learn the art of personal address. Do not let us be so bashful and retiring that we leave others in sorrow because we cannot raise up our courage to say a kind and tender word in the name of the Lord Jesus. Come, let us pluck up courage and encourage every Ruth when she is timid among strangers. Let us help her to feel at home in Immanuel's land!

The new convert is like Ruth in another respect—he is very low in his own eyes. Ruth said to Boaz, "Why have I found grace in your eyes, that you should take knowledge of me, seeing I am a stranger?" She said again, "Let me find favor in your sight, my lord, because you have comforted me and because you have spoken friendly unto your handmaid, though I am not like one of your handmaidens." She had little self-esteem and, therefore, she won the esteem of others. She felt herself to be a very insignificant person, to whom any kindness was a great favor—and so do young converts, if they are real and true. We meet with a certain class of them who are rather pert and forward, as the fashion of the day is in certain quarters, and then we do not think so much of them as they do of themselves! But the genuine ones, who are truly renewed, who really hold out and continue to the end, are always humble.

And frequently they are very trembling, timid and diffident. They feel that they are not worthy to be put among the children and they come to the Lord's Table with holy wonder. I remember when I first went to the house of God as a Christian youth who had lately come to know the Lord. I looked with veneration on every officer and member of the Church! I thought them all, if not quite angels, yet very nearly as good! At any rate, I had no disposition to criticize them, for I felt myself to be so undeserving. I do not think that I have quite so high an idea of all professed Christians as I had, then, for I am afraid that I could not truthfully entertain it. But, for all that, I think far better of them than many are apt to do. I believe that young people, when first brought to Christ, have so deep a sense of their own imperfection and know so little of the infirmities of others, that they look up to the members of the Church with a very high esteem—and this fixes upon such members, officers and pastors a great responsibility. Since these converts are lowly in their own eyes, it is proper and safe to encourage them.

Moreover, it is kind and necessary to do. Never be critical and severe with them, but deal tenderly with their budding gifts—a frosty sentence may nip them—a genial word will develop them. Our Lord bids you feed the lambs. Act the shepherd towards them and never overdrive them, lest they faint by the way. It is a lovely sight to see a matronly Christian cheering on her class of girls, bearing with their waywardness and folly, and fostering everything that is hopeful in them. These are the mothers in Israel to whom shall be honor! I love to see the advanced man of God giving a hearty grip to a youth, loving him, advising him—yes, and adding a word of praise when it can be judiciously applied. With unequal footsteps the raw recruits are trying to keep step with the better-trained soldiers. Let their comrades smile upon them and see in them the warriors of the future who shall rally to the standard when our warfare is ended.

Once more, the young convert is like Ruth because he has come to trust under the wings of Jehovah, the God of Israel. Here is a beautiful metaphor. You know that the wings of a strong bird, especially, and of any bird relatively, is strong. It makes a kind of arch and from the outer side you have the architectural idea of strength. Under the wings, even of so feeble a creature as a hen, there is a complete and perfect refuge for her little chicks, judging from without. And then the inside of the wing is lined with soft feathers for the comfort of the young. The interior of the wing is arranged as though it would prevent any friction from the strength of the wing to the weakness of the little bird. I do not know of a more snug place than under the wing feathers of the hen. Have you ever thought of this?

Would not the Lord have us, in time of trouble, come and cower down under the great wing of His Omnipotent Love, just as the chicks do under the mother? Here is the Scripture—"He shall cover you with His feathers, and under His wings shall you trust: His truth shall be your shield and buckler." What a warm defense! When I have seen the little birds stick their heads out from under the feathers of their mother's breast, it has looked like the perfection of happiness! And when they have chirped their little notes, they have seemed to tell her how warm and safe they were, though there may have been a rough wind blowing around the hen. They could not be happier than they are! If they run a little way, they are soon back, again, to the wing, for it is house and home to them—it is their shield and succor, defense and delight!

This is what our young converts have done. They have come, not to trust themselves, but to trust in Jesus. They have come to find a righteousness in Christ—yes, to find everything in Him—and so they are trusting, trusting under the wings of God! Is not this what you are doing? You full-grown saints—is not this your condition? I know it is! Very well, then, encourage the younger sort to do what you delight to do! Say to them, "There is no place like this. Let us joyously abide together under the wings of God." There is no rest, no peace, no calm, no perfect quiet like that of giving up all care because you cast your care on God, renouncing all fear because your only fear is a fear of offending God! Oh the bliss of knowing that sooner may the universe be dissolved than the great heart that beats above you cease to be full of tenderness and love to all those that shelter beneath it! Faith, however little, is a precious garden of the Lord's right hand planting—do not trample on it, but tend it with care and water it with love.

II. But now I must come closer to the text. Having shown you what these converts have done to need encouragement,

I need, in the second place, to answer the question, WHAT IS THE FULL REWARD OF THOSE WHO COME TO TRUST UNDER THE WINGS OF GOD?

I would answer that a full reward will come to us in that day when we lay down these bodies of flesh and blood, that they may sleep in Jesus, while our unclothed spirits are absent from the body but present with the Lord. In the disembodied state, we shall enjoy perfect happiness of spirit. But a fuller reward will be ours when the Lord shall come a second time and our bodies shall rise from the grave to share in the glorious reign of the descended King! Then, in our perfect manhood, we shall behold the face of Him we love and shall be like He! Then shall come the adoption, to wit, the redemption of our body and we, as body, soul and spirit—a trinity in unity—shall be forever with Father, Son and Holy Spirit—our triune God! This unspeakable bliss is the full reward of trusting beneath the wings of Jehovah!

But there is a present reward and to that Boaz referred. There is, in this world, a present recompense for the godly, notwithstanding the fact that many are true afflictions of the righteous. Years ago a brother minister printed a book, *How to Make the Best of Both Worlds*, which contained much wisdom. But, at the same time, many of us objected to the title as dividing the pursuit of the Believer and putting the two worlds too much on a level. Assuredly, it would be wrong for any godly man to make it his objective in life to make the best of both worlds in the way which the title is likely to suggest. This present world must be subordinate to the world to come and is to be cheerfully sacrificed to it if necessary. Yet, be it never forgotten, if any man will live unto God, he will make the best of both worlds, for godliness has the promise of the life that now is as well as of that which is to come. Even in losing the present life for Christ's sake, we are saving it—and self-denial and taking up the Cross are but forms of blessedness. If we seek, first, the

Kingdom of God and His righteousness, all other things shall be added to us!

Do you ask me, "How shall we be rewarded for trusting in the Lord?" I answer, first, by the deep peace of conscience which He will grant you. Can any reward be better than this? When a man can say, "I have sinned, but I am forgiven," is not that forgiveness an unspeakable reward? My sins were laid on Jesus and He took them away as my Scapegoat, so that they are gone forever and I am consciously absolved. Is not this a glorious assurance? Is it not worth worlds? A calm settles down upon the heart which is under the power of the blood of sprinkling! A voice within proclaims the peace of God and the Holy Spirit seals that peace by His own witness—and thus all is rest. If you were to offer all that you have, to buy this peace, you could not purchase it! And were it purchasable, it were worthwhile to forego the dowry of a myriad worlds to have it! If you had all riches and power and honor you could not reach the price of the Pearl of Peace!

The revenues of kingdoms could not purchase so much as a glance at this jewel. A guilty conscience is the undying worm of Hell. The torture of remorse is the fire that never can be quenched. He that has that worm gnawing at his heart and that fire burning in his bosom is already lost. On the other hand, he that trusts in God through Christ Jesus is delivered from inward Hell-pangs and the burning fever of unrest is cured. He may well sing for joy of soul, for Heaven is born within him and lies in his heart like the Christ in the manger. O harps of Glory, you ring out no sweeter note than that of transgression put away by the atoning Sacrifice!

That, however, is only the beginning of the Believer's reward. He that has come to trust in God shall be "quiet from fear of evil." What a blessing that must be! "He shall not be afraid of evil tidings; his heart is fixed, trusting in the Lord." When a man is at his very highest as to this world's joy, he hears the whisper of a dark spirit saying, "Will it last?" He peers into the morning with apprehension, for he knows not what may be lurking in his path. But when a man is no longer afraid, but is prepared to welcome whatever comes because he sees in it the appointment of a loving Father, why, then he is in a happy state! Suppose one went home tonight and found, as Job did, that all his estate had been burned or stolen and that his family had all died? What a splendid condition must he be in if he could say amid his natural agony, "The Lord gave and the Lord has taken away; blessed be the name of the Lord"! Such possession of the soul in patience is one of the full rewards of faith. He that has it wears a nobler decoration within his breast than all the stars that royalty could bestow! Deliverance from the pangs of conscience and freedom from the griefs of fear make up a choice favor such as only God can give!

More than this—the man who trusts in God rests in Him with respect to all the supplies he now needs, or shall ever need. What happy music gladdens the green pastures of that 23rd Psalm! I am half inclined to ask you to rise and sing it, for my heart is leaping for joy while I rehearse the first stanza of it—

> "The Lord my Shepherd is:
> I shall be well supplied.
> Since He is mine and I am His,
> What can I need beside?"

Usually man is made up of needs—and he must have reached the land of abounding wealth who boldly asks, "What can I need beside?" We are never quite content. It always needs a little more to fill the cup to the brim, but only think of singing, "What can I need beside?" Is not this sweet content a full reward from the Lord in whom we trust? Human nature has swallowed a horseleech and, therefore, it cries night and day, "Give, give, give!" Who but the Lord can satisfy this craving? The vortex of dissatisfaction threatens to suck in the main ocean and still to remain unfilled, but the Lord rewards faith by satisfying its mouth with good things and making it sing—

> "What need shall not our God supply,
> From His redundant stores?

> What streams of mercy from on high
> An arm almighty pours!"

I cannot imagine a fuller present reward than complete rest from all anxiety and calm confidence in a Providence which ran never fail!

Another part of the Believer's great gain lies in the consciousness that all things are working together for His good. Nothing is, after all, able to injure us. Neither pains of body, nor sufferings of mind, nor losses in business, nor cruel blows of death can work us real ill. The thefts of robbers, the mutterings of slanderers, the changes of trade, the rage of the elements shall all be overruled for good! These many drugs and poisons, compounded in the mortar of the unerring Chemist, shall produce a healthy potion for our souls! "We know that all things work together for good to them that love God, to them who are the called according to His purpose." It is a great joy to know this to be an unquestionable fact and to watch, with expectation, to see it repeated in our own case. It takes the sting out, at once, of all these wasps that otherwise would have worried us. And it transforms them into bees, each one gathering honey for us! Is not this a reward for which a man may well forego the flatteries of sin? O Faith, you enrich and ennoble all who entertain you!

Then, let me tell you, they that trust in God and follow Him have another full reward and that is, the bliss of doing good. Can any happiness excel this? This joy is a diamond of the first water! Match me, if you can, the joy of helping the widow and the fatherless! Find me the equal of the delight of saving a soul from death and covering a multitude of sins! It were worth worlds to have faith in God, even if we lived here forever, if our sojourn could be filled up with doing good to the poor and needy and rescuing the erring and fallen. If you desire to taste the purest joy that ever flowed from the fountains of Paradise, drink of the unselfish bliss of saving a lost soul! When faith in God teaches you to forego self and live wholly to glorify God and benefit your fellow men, it puts you on the track of the Lord of angels and, by following it, you will come to reign with Him.

There has lately passed away from our midst on this side of the river one who, in his earlier days, knew the curse of drunkenness, but was led, by hearing the Gospel in the street, to seek and find a Savior and so to escape from the bondage of an evil habit. He became a Christian temperance man, devoting himself—I was about to say every day in the week, to the cause—for I think he did so! All his spare time was spent for that sacred purpose. He has lately passed away, but not without having enjoyed a reward from his God. When I used to look into the face of our friend, Mr. Thorniloe, I felt that he had received a full return for casting himself upon the Lord, for the joy of his heart shone in his countenance and delight in his work caused it to be his recreation! O drunk, if you could become such as he was, total abstinence would be no trial, but a pleasure! O idle professor, if you would be as diligent in serving your Lord as he was, life would be music to you! He who has, himself, fallen into a sin, should find his chief joy in seeking to reclaim others from the same condemnation. And in doing so, he will light upon clouds of happiness and flocks of joys! As a shepherd rejoices most when he has found his straying sheep, so will you who trust in the Lord, if you will, in the future, lay yourselves out to pluck men from eternal ruin.

Brothers and Sisters, there remains the singular and refined joy which comes of a humble perception of personal growth. Children rejoice when they find that they are growing more like their parents and may soon hope to be strong and full-grown. Most of us remember our childish mirth when we began to wear garments which we thought would make us look like men! When I first wore boots and walked through the stubble with my big uncle, I felt that I was somebody! That, of course, was childish pride—but it has its commendable analogy in the pleasure of gathering spiritual strength and becoming equal to higher labors and deeper experiences! When you find that you do not lose your temper under provocation, as you did a year ago, you are humbly thankful. When an evil lust is driven away and no longer haunts you, you are quietly joyful, rejoicing with trembling. When you have sustained a trial which once would have crushed you, the victory is exceedingly sweet. Every advance in holiness is an advance in secret happiness! To be a little more meet for Heaven is to have a little more of Heaven in the heart! As we mellow for the celestial garner, we are conscious of a more pervading sweetness which, in itself, is no mean reward of virtue.

Let me tell you another splendid part of this full reward, and that is to have prevalence with God in prayer. Somebody called me, in print, a hypocrite, because I said that God had heard my prayers. This was evidently malicious—a man might be called fanatical for such a statement, but I cannot see the justice of imputing hypocrisy on that account! If by hypocrisy he meant a sincere conviction that the great God answers prayer, I will be more and more hypocritical as long as I live! I will glory in the name of God—the God That Hears My Prayer! If that writer had claimed that he prayed and had been heard, it is possible that he would have been guilty of hypocrisy—of that matter, he is personally the best informed, and I leave the question with him. But he has no right to measure my corn with his bushel. Certainly, I shall not use his bushel to measure my corn, but I shall speak what I know and am persuaded of! In deep sincerity I can bear testimony that the Lord hears prayer and that it is His desire to do so!

Many a saint of God has but to ask and have. When such men wrestle with God in prayer, they always prevail like Israel of old at Jabbok, when he grasped the Angel and would not let Him go without a blessing. If you have got this power to the fullest, you will often say to yourself, "If I have nothing else but power at the Throne of Grace, I have more than enough to recompense me for every self-denial." What are the jests and jeers of an ungodly and ignorant world in comparison with the honor of being favored of the Lord to ask what we will and receive the utmost of our desires?

Many other items make up the full of the reward, but perhaps the chief of all is communion with God—to be permitted to speak with Him as a man speaks with his friend—to be led by the Divine Bridegroom to sit down in the banqueting house while His banner over us is Love. Those who dwell outside the palace of Love know nothing about our secret ecstasies and raptures. We cannot tell them much about our spiritual delights, for they would only turn, again, and tear us. The delights of heavenly fellowship are too sacred to be commonly displayed. There is a joy, the clearest example of Heaven below, when the soul becomes as the chariot of Amminadib by the energy of the Holy Spirit! I believe, Brothers and Sisters, that our lot, even when we are poor and sorrowful and cast down, is infinitely to be preferred to that of the loftiest emperor who does not know the Savior!

Oh, poor kings, poor princes, poor peers, poor gentry that do not know Christ! But happy paupers that know Him! Happy slaves that love Him! Happy dying men and women that rejoice in Him! Those have solid joy and lasting pleasure who have God to be their All in All. Come, then, and put your trust under the wings of God and you shall be blessed in your body and in your soul! You shall be blessed in your house and in your family! You shall be blessed in your basket and in your store—blessed in your sickness and in your health, blessed in time and in eternity—for the righteous are blessed of the Lord and their offspring with them!

My prayer for every young convert is the benediction of Boaz, "The Lord recompense your work, and a full reward be given you of the Lord God of Israel, under whose wings you are come to trust." May this benediction rest on each one of you forever.

III. Finally, WHAT FIGURE SETS FORTH THIS FULL REWARD? What was the full reward that Ruth obtained? I do not think that Boaz knew the full meaning of what he said. He could not foresee all that was appointed of the Lord. In the light of Ruth's history, we will read the good man's blessing. This poor stranger, Ruth, in coming to put her trust in the God of Israel, was giving up everything. Yes, but she was also gaining everything. If she could have looked behind the veil which hides the future, she could not have conducted herself more to her own advantage than she did! She had no prospect of gain. She followed Naomi expecting poverty and obscurity, but, in doing that which was right, she found the blessing which makes rich! She lost her Moabite kindred, but she found a noble kinsman in Israel. She left the home of her fathers in the other land to find a heritage among the chosen tribes, a heritage redeemed by one who loved her! Ah, when you come to trust in Christ, you find, in the Lord Jesus Christ, One who is next of kin to you, who redeems your heritage and unites you to Himself! You thought that He was a stranger. You were afraid to approach Him, but He comes near to you and you find yourself near to His heart and one with Him forever.

Yes, this is a fair picture of each convert's reward. Ruth found what she did not look for. She found a husband. It was exactly what was for her comfort and her joy, for she found rest in the house of her husband and she became possessed of his large estate by virtue of her marriage union with him. When a poor sinner trusts in God, he does not expect so

great a reward, but, to his surprise, his heart finds a husband, a home and an inheritance priceless beyond all conception—and all this is found in Christ Jesus our Lord! Then is the soul brought into loving, living, lasting, indissoluble union with the Well-Beloved, the unrivalled Lord of Love! We are one with Jesus! What a glorious mystery is this!

Ruth obtained an inheritance among the chosen people of Jehovah. She could not have obtained it except through Boaz, who redeemed it for her, but thus she came into indisputable possession of it. When a poor soul comes to God, he thinks that he is flying to Him only for a refuge, but, indeed, he is coming for much more. He is coming for an undefiled heritage that fades not. He becomes an heir of God, a joint-heir with Jesus Christ!

As I conclude, I bear this, my personal testimony, to the benefit of godliness for this life. Apart from the glories of Heaven, I would wish to live trusting in my God and resting in Him for this present life since I need His present aid for every day as truly as I shall need it at the last day. Men speak of secularism as attending to the things which concern our present life and I am bold to assert that the purest and best secularism is that which trusts itself with God for things immediately around us! We shall be wise to make secular things sacred by trusting them with God. Faith is not for eternity, alone, but for this fleeting hour, also—it is good for the shop and for the marketplace—for the field and for the domestic hearth. For the cares of the moment, as well as for everything else, we take refuge under the wings of God! There shall we be blessed, for Christ's sake. Amen.

4
MEALTIME IN THE CORN FIELDS

"And Boaz said unto her, At mealtime come you here and eat of the bread and dip your morsel in the vinegar. And she sat beside the reapers: and he reached her parched corn and she did eat and was sufficed and left."

—Ruth 2:14

IF WE LIVED IN THE country it would not be necessary for me to remind you that the time of harvest has again happily come upon us. I saw, one day last week, a fine sample of the new wheat, part of a considerable quantity which had just been sold. And in many places I have observed the fields yielding their sheaves to the reapers' sickle. Let us loudly lift our praises to God for the abundance which loads the land. An unusually heavy crop has been given in many quarters and scarcely anywhere is there any deficiency.

While there is so much of distress abroad—while the great factories of our country are standing still—we should be grateful that God is pleased to alleviate the sufferings of the poor by an unusually bountiful harvest. And we must not forget to pray that during the next few weeks the Lord would be pleased to give suitable weather so that the corn may be safely gathered into the garner. That there may be abundance of bread and no complaining in our streets. I always feel it necessary, just at this season, to give these hints, because God's natural remembrances cannot reach us—we hear not the lark teaching us how to praise, nor do the green fields of grass, and the yellow ears of corn preach to us of the Lord's bounty.

Little is there to be learned from these long corridors of dreary cells which we call streets and houses. I see dull brown or dirty-white bricks everywhere—enough to make one earthly—however much we may pant for heavenly things. We see neither the green blade nor the full corn in the ear, and we are so apt to forget that we all depend upon the labor of the field. Let us unite with the peasant and his master in blessing and praising the God of Providence, who first covered the fields with grass for the cattle and now with herbs for the food of man.

This morning we are going to the corn fields, as we did last year, not however, so much to glean, as to rest with the reapers and the gleaners, when under some wide-spreading oak they sit down to take refreshment. We hope there will be found some timid gleaner here who will accept our invitation to come and eat with us, and who will find confidence enough to dip their morsel in the vinegar. May they have courage to feast to the full on their own account, and then to carry home a portion to their needy friends at home.

I. Our first point this morning is this—THAT GOD'S REAPERS HAVE THEIR MEALTIMES. Those who work for God will find Him a good Master. He cares for oxen, and has commanded His Israel, "You shall not muzzle the ox when he treads out the corn." Much more does He care for His servants who serve Him. "He has given meat unto them that fear Him: He will ever be mindful of His Covenant." The reapers in Jesus' fields shall not only receive a blessed reward at the last, but they shall have plenteous comforts by the way.

He is pleased to pay His servants twice—first in the labor itself—and a second time in the labor's sweet results. He gives them such joy and consolation in the service of their Master that it is a sweet employ, and they cry, "We delight to do Your will, O Lord." As Heaven is made up of serving God day and night, so to true workers, their constantly serving God on earth brings with it a rich foretaste of Heaven.

God has ordained certain mealtimes for His reapers. And He has appointed that one of these shall be when they come together to listen to the Word preached. If God is with our ministers, they act as the disciples did of old. They received the barley loaves and fishes from

Christ, and handed them to the people as He multiplied them. We, of ourselves, cannot feed one soul, much less thousands. But when the Lord is with us, we can keep as good a table as Solomon himself, with all his fine flour, fat, roebucks, and small deer.

When the Lord blesses the provisions of His House, no matter how many thousands there may be, all His poor shall be filled with bread. I hope, Beloved, you know what it is to sit under the shadow of the Word with great delight and find the fruit sweet unto your taste. Where the Doctrines of Grace are boldly and plainly delivered to you in connection with the other Truths of Revelation. Where Jesus Christ upon His Cross is always lifted up. Where the work of the Spirit is not forgotten. Where the glorious purpose of the Father is never despised—there is sure to be food for the children of God.

We have learned not to feed upon oratorical flourishes or philosophical fineries. We leave these fine things, these twelfth-cake ornaments, to be eaten by those little children who can find delight in such unhealthy dainties—we prefer to hear the Truth of God, even when roughly spoken—to the fine garnishing of eloquence without the Truth. We care little about how the table is served, or of what ware the dishes are made—so long as the Covenant bread and water, and the promised oil and wine are given to us. Certain grumblers among the Lord's reapers do not feed under the preached Word because they do not intend to feed. They come to the House of Bread on purpose to find fault, and therefore they go away empty.

My verdict is, "It serves them right." Little care I to please such hearers. I would as soon feed bears and jackals, as attempt to supply the wants of grumbling professors. How much mischief is done by observations made upon the preacher! How often do we censure where our God approves. We have heard of a high doctrinal deacon who said to a young minister who was supplying the pulpit on probation, "I should have enjoyed your sermon very much, Sir, if it had not been for that last appeal to the sinner. I do not think that dead sinners should be exhorted to believe in Jesus."

When that deacon reached home he found his own daughter in tears. She became converted to God and united with the Church of which that young man ultimately became the minister. How was she converted, do you think? By that address at the close of the sermon, which her father did not like. Take heed of railing at that by which the Holy Spirit saves souls! There may be much in the sermon which may not suit you, or me, but then we are not the only persons to be considered. There is a wide variety of characters and all our hearers must have "their portion of meat in due season."

Is it not a selfishness very unlike the spirit of a Christian which would make me find fault with the provisions, because I cannot eat them all? There should be the unadulterated milk for the babe in Grace, as well as the strong substantial meat for the full grown Believer. Beloved, I know that murmurers may call our manna, "light bread," yet our gracious God does, "in this mountain make unto all people a feast of fat things, a feast of wines on the lees, of fat things full of marrow, of wines on the lees well refined."

Often, too, our gracious Lord appoints us mealtimes in our private readings and meditations. Here it is that His "paths drop fatness." Nothing can be more fattening to the soul of the Believer than feeding upon the Word and digesting it by frequent meditations. No wonder that some grow so little, when they meditate so little. Cattle must chew the cud. It is not what they crop with their teeth, but that which is masticated and afterwards digested by rumination that nourishes them. We must take the Truth of God and roll it over and over again in the inward parts of our spirit, and so we shall extract Divine nourishment from it.

Have you not, my Brothers and Sisters, frequently found a Benjamin's mess prepared for you in a choice promise of your God? Is not meditation the land of Goshen to you? If men once said, "There is corn in Egypt," may they not always say that the finest of the wheat is to be found in secret prayer? Private devotion is a land which flows with milk and honey—a Paradise yielding all manner of fruits—a banqueting house of choice wines. Ahasuerus might make a great feast, but all his hundred and twenty provinces could not furnish such dainties as the closet offers to the spiritual mind! Where can we feed and lie down in green pastures in so sweet a sense as we do in our musings on the Word?

Meditation distils the quintessence from the Scriptures and gladdens our mouth with a sweetness which exceeds the virgin honey dropping from the honeycomb. Your retired seasons and occasions of prayer should be to you regal entertainments, or at least refreshing seasons, in which, like the reapers at noonday, you sit with Boaz and eat of your Master's generous provisions. "The Shepherd of Salisbury Plain"—you who have read that excellent book will remember—was custom to say, "that when he was lonely and when his wallet was empty, his Bible was to him meat and drink and company, too." He is not the only man who has found a fullness in the Word when there is want without.

During the battle of Waterloo a godly soldier, mortally wounded, was carried by his comrade into the rear, and being placed with his back propped up against a tree, he besought his friend to open his knapsack and take out the Bible which he had carried in it. "Read to me," he said, "one verse, before I close my eyes in death." His comrade read him that verse—"Peace I leave with you, my peace I give unto you: not as the world gives, give I unto you." And there, fresh from the whistling of the bullets, the roll of the drum, and the tempest of human conflict, that believing spirit enjoyed such holy calm that before he fell asleep in the arms of Jesus, he said, "Yes, I have a peace with God which passes all understanding, which keeps my heart and mind through Jesus Christ." Saints most surely have their mealtimes when they are alone in meditation.

Let us not forget that there is one specially ordained mealtime which ought to occur oftener, but which, even monthly, is very refreshing to us. I mean the Supper of the Lord. There you have literally, as well as spiritually, a meal. The table is richly spread. It has upon it both meat and drink. There is the bread and the wine, and looking at what these symbolize, we have before us a table richer than that which kings could furnish. There we have the flesh and the blood of our Lord Jesus Christ, of which if a man eats, he shall never hunger and never thirst, for that bread shall be unto him everlasting life.

Oh, the sweet seasons we have known at the Lord's Supper! If some of you really did understand the enjoyment of feeding upon Christ in that ordinance, you would chide yourselves for not having united with the Church in fellowship! In keeping the Master's commandments there is a "great reward," and consequently, in neglecting them there is a great loss of reward. Christ is not so tied to the Sacramental table as to be always found of those who partake there, but still it is in the way that we may expect the Lord to meet with us. "If you love Me, keep My commandments"—it is a sentence of touching power. "And His commandments are not grievous," is the confession of all obedient sons.

Sitting at this table, our soul has mounted up from the emblem to the reality. We have eaten bread in the kingdom of God and have leaned our head upon Jesus' bosom. "He brought me to the banqueting house and His banner over me was love." On these occasions we may compare ourselves to poor Mephibosheth, who though lame and despicable in his own esteem, yet was made to sit at King David's table. Or we may liken ourselves to the little ewe lamb in the parable which did eat of its Master's bread and drink from his cup and slept in his bosom. The prodigal, who once fed upon husks, sits down to eat the bread of children. We, who were worthy to be esteemed as dogs, are here permitted to take the place of adopted sons and daughters.

Besides these regular mealtimes, there are others which God gives us, at seasons when perhaps we little expect them. You have been walking the street and suddenly you have felt a holy flowing out of your soul toward God. Or, in the middle of business your heart has been melted with love and made to leap for joy even as the brooks which have been bound with winter's ice leap to feel the touch of spring. You have been groaning, dull and earth-bound. But the sweet love of Jesus has embraced you when you scarcely thought of it, and your spirit, all free and all on fire, has rejoiced to dance before the Lord with tambourines and high-sounding cymbals, like Miriam of old.

I have had times occasionally in preaching when I would gladly have kept on far beyond the appointed hour, for my happy soul was like a vessel wanting vent. Seasons, too, you have had on your sick-beds when you would have been content to be sick always, if you could have your bed so well made and your head so softly pillowed—

> "These are the joys He lets us know,
> In fields and villages below—
> Gives us a relish of His love,
> But keeps His noble feast above."

Our blessed Redeemer sometimes comes to us in the morning and wakes us up with such sweet thoughts upon our soul, we know not how they came. And when the dew is visiting the flowers in the cool eventide, sometimes a few drops of Heaven's dew falls upon us, too. And as we have gone to our beds, our meditation of Him has been sweet. And in the night watches, when we tossed to and fro and could not sleep, He has been pleased to become our song in the night—

> "He is the spring of all my joys,
> The life of my delights;
> The glory of my brightest days,
> And comfort of my nights."

God's reapers find it hard work to reap. But they find a blessed solace when they sit down and eat of their Master's rich provisions. Then, with renewed strength they go with sharpened sickles to reap again in the noontide heat.

Let me observe that while these mealtimes come, even though we know not exactly when, there are certain seasons when we may expect them. The Eastern reapers generally sit down under the shelter of a tree, or a booth, to take refreshment during the heat of the day. And I am certain that when trouble, affliction, persecution and bereavement become the most painful to us, it is then that the Lord hands out to us the sweetest comforts. As we said last Thursday night, some promises are written in sympathetic ink and can only have their meaning brought out by holding them before the fire of affliction.

Some verses of Scripture must be held to the fire till they are scorched before the glorious meaning will stand forth, in clear letters, before our eyes. We must work till the hot sun forces the sweat from our face. We must bear the burden and heat of the day before we can expect to be invited to those choice meals which the Lord prepares for those who are diligent in His work. When your day of trouble is the hottest, then the love of Jesus shall be sweetest. When your night of trial is the darkest, then will His candle shine most brightly about you. When your head aches most severely. When your heart palpitates most terribly. When heart and flesh fail you—then He will be the strength of your life and your portion forever.

Again, these mealtimes frequently occur before a trial. Elijah must be entertained beneath a juniper tree, for he is to go a forty days' journey in the strength of that meat. You may suspect some danger near when your delights are overflowing. If you see a ship taking in great quantities of provision, it is bound for a distant port. And when God gives you extraordinary seasons of communion with Jesus, you may look for long leagues of tempestuous sea. Sweet cordials prepare us for stern conflicts. Times of refreshing also occur after trouble or arduous service. Christ was tempted by the devil, and afterwards angels came and ministered unto Him.

Jacob wrestled with God and then afterwards, at Mahanaim, hosts of angels met him. Abraham wars with the kings and returns from their slaughter. Then is it that Melchisedek refreshes him with bread and wine. After conflict, content. After battle, banquet. When you have waited on your Lord, then you shall sit down and your Master will gird Himself and wait upon you. Yes, let the worldling say what he will about the hardness of religion, we do not find it so. We do confess that reaping is no child's play—that toiling for Christ has its difficulties and its troubles. But still the bread which we eat is very sweet and the wine which we drink is crushed from celestial clusters—

> "I would not change my blessed estate,
> For all the world calls good or great.
> And while my faith can keep her hold,
> I envy not the sinner's gold."

II. Follow me while we turn to a second point. TO THESE MEALS THE GLEANER IS AFFECTIONATELY INVITED. That is to say, the poor trembling stranger who has not strength enough to reap—who has no right to be in the field, except the right of charity. The poor trembling sinner, conscious of his own demerit and feeling but little hope and little joy. To the meals of the strong-handed, fully-assured reaper, the gleaner is invited. The gleaner is invited, in the text, to come. "At mealtime, come you here." We have known some who felt ashamed to come to the House of God. But we trust you will, none of you, be kept away from the place of feasting by any shame on account of your dress, or your personal character, or your poverty—no, nor even on account of your physical infirmities. "At mealtime come you here."

I have heard of a deaf woman who could never hear a sound, and yet she was always in the House of God. And when asked why, her reply was, "Because a friend found her the text and then God was pleased to give her many a sweet thought upon the text while she sat in his House. Besides," she said, "she felt that as a Believer, she ought to honor God by her presence in His courts, and recognize her union with His people. And, better still, she always liked to be in the best of company. And as the Presence of God was there, and the holy angels and the saints of the Most High—whether she could hear or not—she would go."

There is a Brother whose face I seldom miss from this House. He, I believe, has never in his life heard a sound, and cannot make an articulate utterance Yet he is a joyful Believer and loves the place where God's honor dwells. Well, now, I think if such persons find pleasure in coming, we who can hear, though we feel our unworthiness—though we are conscious that we are not fit to come—should be desirous to be laid in the House of God, as the sick were at the pool of Bethesda, hoping that the waters may be stirred, and that we may step in and be healed. Trembling Soul, never let the temptations of the devil keep you from God's House. "At mealtime come you here."

Moreover, she was bid not only to come, but to eat. Now, whatever there is sweet and comfortable in the Word of God, you that are of a broken and contrite spirit, are invited to partake of it. "Jesus Christ came into the world to save sinners"—sinners such as you are. "In due time Christ died for the ungodly"—for such ungodly ones as you feel yourselves to be. You are desiring, this morning, to be Christ's. Well, you may be Christ's. You are saying in your heart, "O that I could eat the children's bread!" You may eat it. You say, "I have no right." But He gives you the invitation! Come without any other right than the right of His invitation. I know you will say how unworthy you are—

> "Let not conscience make you linger,
> Nor of fitness fondly dream."

But since Christ bids you, "come," take Him at His word. And if there is a promise, believe it. If there is rich consolation, drink it. If there is an encouraging word, accept it and let the sweetness of it be yours. Note further, that she was not only invited to eat the bread, but to dip her morsel in the vinegar. We must not look upon this as being some sour stuff. No doubt there are crabbed souls in the Church who always dip their morsel in the sourest imaginable vinegar and, with a grim liberality, invite others to share a little comfortable misery with them. But the vinegar in my text is altogether another thing.

This was either a compound of various sweets extracted from fruits, or else it was that weak kind of wine mingled with water which is still commonly used in the harvest fields of Italy and the warmer parts of the world—a drink not exceedingly strong, but excellently cooling and good enough to impart a relish to the reapers' food. It was, to use the only word which will give the meaning, a sauce which the Orientals used with their bread. As we use butter, or as they on other occasions used oil, so in the harvest field, believing it to have cooling properties, they used what is here called vinegar.

Beloved, the Lord's reapers have sauce with their bread. They have sweet consolations. They have not merely doctrines, but the holy unction which is the essence of doctrines. They have not merely the Truths of God, but a hallowed and ravishing delight accompanies the Truths. Take, for instance, the doctrine of election, which is like the bread. There is a sauce to dip that in. When I can say, "He loved me before the foundations of the world," the personal application, the personal enjoyment of my interest in the Truth of God becomes a sauce into which I dip my morsel.

And you, poor Gleaner, are invited to dip your morsel in it, too. I used to hear people sing that hymn of Toplady's, which begins—

> "A debtor to mercy alone,
> Of Covenant mercy I sing;
> Nor fear with Your righteousness on,
> My person and offerings to bring."

And rises to its climax—

> "Yes, I to the end shall endure,
> As sure as the earnest is given;
> More happy, but not more secure,
> The glorified spirits in Heaven."

And I used to think I could never sing that hymn. It was the sauce, you know. I might manage to eat some of the plain bread, but I could not dip it in that sauce. It was too high doctrine, too sweet, too consoling. But I thank God I have since ventured to dip my morsel in it and now I hardly like my bread without it.

I would have every trembling sinner be prepared to take the comfortable parts of God's Word, even those called "HIGH." I hope, Brothers and Sisters, you will never grow as some Christians do—who like all sauce and no bread. There are some high-flying Brothers and Sisters who must have nothing but the vinegar. And very sour it turns upon their stomachs, too. I hope you will love the bread. A little of the vinegar, a little of the spice, and much savor. But let us keep to the bread as well. Let us love all revealed Truth of God. And if there is a trembling gleaner here, let me invite and persuade her to come here, to eat the bread and to dip her morsel in the sauce.

Now I think I see her and she is half prepared to come. She is very hungry, and she has brought nothing with her this morning. But she begins to say, "I have no right to come, for I am not a reaper. I do nothing for Christ. I did not even come here this morning to honor Him. I came here, as gleaners go into a corn field, from a selfish motive, to pick up what

I could for myself. And all the religion that I have lies in this—the hope that I may be saved. I do not glorify God. I do no good to other people. I am only a selfish gleaner. I am not a reaper."

Ah, but you are invited to come. Make no questions about it. Boaz bids you. Take his invitation and enter at once. But, you say, "I am such a poor gleaner. Though it is all for myself, yet it is little I get at it. I get a few thoughts while the sermon is being preached, but I lose them before I reach home." I know you do, poor weak-handed Woman. But still, Jesus invites you. Come! Take the sweet promise as He presents it to you, and let no bashfulness of yours send you home hungry. "But," you say, "I am a stranger. You do not know my sins, my sinfulness, and the waywardness of my heart."

But Jesus does. And Jesus still invites you! He knows you are but a Moabitess, a stranger from the commonwealth of Israel. But He bids you! Is not that enough? "Eat the bread and dip your morsel in the vinegar." "But," you say, "I owe so much to Him already. It is so good of Him to spare my forfeited life and so tender of Him to let me hear the Gospel preached at all. I cannot have the presumption to be an intruder and sit with the reapers." Oh, but He bids you. There is more presumption in your doubting than there could be in your believing. HE bids you! Will you refuse Boaz? Shall Jesus' lips give the invitation, and will you say no?

Come, now, come. Remember that the little which Ruth could eat did not make Boaz any the poorer. And all that you want will make Christ none the less glorious, or full of Grace. What? Are your necessities large? Yes? But His supplies are larger! Do you require great mercy? He is a great Savior. I tell you that His mercy is no more to be exhausted than the sea is to be drained. Or than the sun is to be rendered dim by the excess of the light which he pours forth today. Come! There is enough for you, and Boaz will not be hurt by what you get.

Moreover, let me tell you a secret—Jesus loves you. Therefore it is that He would have you feed at His table. If you are now a longing, trembling sinner, willing to be saved, but conscious that you deserve it not, Jesus loves you, Sinner, and He will take more delight in seeing you eat than you will take in the eating! Let the sweet love He feels in His soul toward you draw you to Him. And what is more—but this is a great secret and must only be whispered in your ear—He intends to be married to you. And when you are married to Him, why, the fields will be yours! For, of course, if you are the spouse, you are joint-proprietor with Him.

Is it not so? Does not the wife share with the husband? All those promises which are, "yes, and Amen in Christ" shall be yours—no, they all are yours NOW, for, "the man is next of kin unto you," and before long He will spread His skirt over you and take you unto Himself forever, espousing you in faithfulness and truth and righteousness. Will you not eat of your own? "Oh, but," says one, "how can it be? I am a stranger." Yes, a stranger—but Jesus Christ loves the stranger. "A publican, a sinner." But He is "the Friend of publicans and sinners." "An outcast." But He "gathers together the outcasts of Israel." "A stray sheep." But the Shepherd "leaves the ninety and nine" to seek it. "A lost piece of money." But He "sweeps the house" to find you. "A prodigal son." But He sets the bells a ringing when He knows that you will return. Come, Ruth! Come, trembling Gleaner! Jesus invites you—accept the invitation. "At mealtime come you here and eat of the bread and dip your morsel in the vinegar."

III. Now, thirdly—and here is a very sweet point in the narrative. BOAZ REACHED HER THE PARCHED CORN. "She did come and eat." Where did she sit? You notice she "sat beside the reapers." She did not feel that she was one of them—she "sat beside" them. Just as some of you do, who do not come down in the evening to the Lord's Supper, but sit in the gallery. You are sitting "beside the reapers." You are sitting this morning as if you were not one of us— had no right to be among the people of God—still you will sit beside us.

If there is a good thing to be had and you cannot get it, you will get as near as you can to those who do. You think there is some comfort even in looking on at the gracious feast. "She sat beside the reapers." And while she was sitting there, what happened? Did she stretch forth her hand and get the food herself? No, it is written, "HE reached her the parched corn." Ah, that is it. I give the invitation, Brothers and Sisters, today—give it earnestly, affectionately, sincerely. But I know very well that while I give it, no trembling heart will accept it unless the King Himself comes near and feasts His saints today.

He must reach the parched corn. He must give you to drink of "the juice of the spiced wine of His pomegranate." How does He do this? By His gracious Spirit. He first of all inspires your faith. You are afraid to think it can be true, that such a sinner as you is accepted in the Beloved. He breathes upon you, and your faint hope becomes an expectancy—and that expectation buds and blossoms into an appropriating faith, which says, "Yes, my Beloved is mine, and His desire is toward me." Having done this, the Savior does more. He sheds abroad the love of God in your heart. The love of Christ is like sweet perfume in a box.

Now, He who put the perfume in the box is the only Person that knows how to take the lid off. He, with His own skillful hands, takes the lid from the box. Then it is, "shed abroad," like "ointment poured forth." You know it may be there, and yet not be shed abroad. As you walk in the woods there may be a hare or a partridge there, and yet you may never see them. But when you startle them, and they fly or run before you, then you perceive them. And there may be the love of God in your heart, not in exercise, but still there. And at last you may have the privilege of seeing it—seeing your love mount with wings to Heaven, and your faith running without weariness. Christ must shed abroad that love—His Spirit must put your Graces into exercise.

But Jesus does more than this. He reaches the parched corn with His own hands when He gives us close communion with Him. Do not think that this is a dream! I tell you there is such a thing as talking with Christ today. As certainly as I can talk with my dearest friend, or find solace in the company of my beloved wife, so surely may I speak with Jesus, and find intense delight in the company of Immanuel. It is not a fiction! We do not worship a far-off Savior. He is a God near at hand. We do not adore Him as One who is gone away to Heaven, and who never can be approached. But He is near us, in our mouth, and in our heart. And we do, today, walk with Him as the elect did of old—and commune with Him as His Apostles did on earth—not after the flesh, it is true, but spiritual men value spiritual communion—better than any carnal fellowship.

Yet once more let me add the Lord Jesus is pleased to reach the parched corn, in the best sense, when the Spirit gives us the infallible witness within, that we are "born of God." A man may know that he is a Christian infallibly. Philip de Morny, who lived in the time of Prince Henry of Navarre, was accustomed to say that the Holy Spirit had made his own salvation to him as clear a point as ever a problem proved to a demonstration in Euclid could be. You know with what mathematical precision the scholar of Euclid solves a problem or proves a proposition! And just the same, with as absolute a precision, as certainly as twice two are four, we may, "know that we have passed from death unto life." The sun in the heavens is not more clear to the eye than his own salvation to an assured Believer—such a man would as soon doubt his own existence, as suspect his interest in eternal life!

Now let the prayer be breathed by poor Ruth, who is trembling yonder. Lord, reach me the parched corn! "Draw me, we will run after You." Lord, send Your love into my heart—

> "Come, Holy Spirit, heavenly Dove,
> With all Your quickening powers,
> Come, shed abroad a Savior's love,
> And that shall kindle ours."

There is no getting at Christ, except by Christ revealing Himself to us.

IV. And now the last point. After Boaz had reached the parched corn, we are told that, "SHE DID EAT, AND WAS SUFFICED, AND LEFT." So shall it be with every Ruth. Sooner or later every penitent shall become a Believer. There may be a space of deep conviction and a period of much hesitation. But, by God's Grace, there shall come a season when the soul decides for the Lord. If I perish, I perish. I will go as I am to Jesus. I will not play the fool any longer with my buts and ifs. Since He bids me believe that He died for me, I will believe it, and will trust His Cross for my salvation. And oh, whenever you shall be privileged to do this, you shall be "satisfied." "She did eat and was satisfied."

Your head shall be satisfied with the precious Truth which Christ reveals. Your heart shall be content with Jesus, as the altogether lovely Object of affection. Your hope shall be satisfied, for whom have you in Heaven but Christ? Your desires shall be satiated, for what can even the hunger of your desire wish for more than "to know Christ and to be found in Him?" You shall find Jesus fills your conscience till it is at perfect peace. He shall fill your judgment till you know the certainty of His teachings. He shall fill your memory with recollections of what He did, and fill your imagination with the prospects of what He is yet to do. You shall be "satisfied." Still, still it shall be true, that you shall leave something. "She was satisfied and she left."

Some of us have had deep draughts. We have thought that we could take in all of Christ. But when we have done our best, we have had to leave a vast remainder. We have sat down with a ravenous appetite at the table of the Lord's love and said, "Now, nothing but the infinite can ever satisfy me. I am such a great sinner that I must have infinite merit to wash my sin away." But we have had our sin removed and found that there was merit to spare. We have had our hunger relieved and found that there was a redundancy for others who were in a similar case.

There are certain sweet things in the Word of God which you and I have not enjoyed yet, and which we cannot enjoy yet. We are obliged to leave them for a while. "I have yet many things to say unto you, but you cannot hear them now." There is a knowledge to which we have not attained—a place of fellowship nearer yet to Christ. There are heights of communion which as yet our feet have not climbed—virgin snows upon the mountain untrod by the foot of man. There is yet a beyond, and there will be a forever.

But please notice—it is not in the text, but it is recorded a verse or two further on, what she did with her leavings. It is a very bad habit, I believe, at feasts, to carry anything home with you. But she did, for that which was left she took home. And when she reached Naomi and showed her the quantity of wheat in her apron, after she had asked, "Where have you gleaned today?" and had received the answer, she gave to Naomi a portion of that which she had reserved after she was sufficed. So it shall be even with you, poor Tremblers, who think you have no right to any for yourselves. You shall be able to eat and be quite satisfied—and what is more—you shall have a morsel to carry to others in a like condition.

I am always pleased to find the young Believer beginning to pocket something for other people. When you hear a sermon, you think, "Well, poor mother cannot get out today, I will tell her something about it. There now, that point will just suit her. I will take that, even if I forget everything else. I will tell her that by the bedside. There is my brother William, who will not come with me to Chapel. I wish he would. But now, there was something which struck me in the sermon and when I get close to him, I will tell him that. Then I will ask, 'Will you not come this evening?' I will tell him those portions which interested me. Perhaps they will interest him."

There are your children in the Sunday school class. You say, "That illustration will do for them." I think sometimes—when I see you putting down my metaphors on little scraps of paper—that you may remember to tell somebody else. I would gladly give more where they are so well used. I would let fall an extra handful on purpose, that there may be enough for you and for your friends. There is an abominable spirit of self among some professors, prompting them to eat their morsels alone. They get the honey. It is a forest full of honey, like Jonathan's woods. And yet they are afraid—afraid lest they should eat it all up—so they try to maintain a monopoly.

I know some congregations which seem, to me, to be sort of spiritual protectionists. They are afraid Heaven will be too full, that there will not be room enough for them. When an invitation is given to a sinner, they do not like it—it is too open, too general. And when there is a melting heart and a tearful eye for the conversion of other people, they feel quite out of their element. They never know what it is to take home that which is left and give to others. Cultivate an unselfish spirit. Seek to love as you have been loved. Remember that "the Law and the Prophets" lie in this—to "love the Lord your God with all your heart and your neighbor as yourself."

How can you love your neighbor as yourself if you do not love his soul? You have loved your own soul—through Divine Grace you have been led to lay hold on Jesus. Love your neighbor's soul, and never be satisfied till you see him in the enjoyment of those things which are the charm of your life and the joy of your spirit. I do not know how to give my invitation in a more comfortable way. But as we are sitting down to feed at His Table in the evening of this day, I pray the Master to reach a large handful of parched corn to some trembling sinner, and enable him to eat and be satisfied.

5
SPIRITUAL GLEANING

"Let her glean even among the sheaves, and reproach her not."

—Ruth 2:15

OUR COUNTRY COUSINS HAVE BEEN engaged recently in harvest occupations and most of them understand what is meant by gleaning. Perhaps they are not, all of them, so wise as to understand the heavenly art of spiritual gleaning. That is the subject which I have chosen for our meditation on this occasion—my attention having been called to it while I have been riding along through the country and, as I like to improve the seasons of the year as they come and go, I shall give you a few homely remarks with regard to spiritual gleaning. In the first place, we shall observe that there is a great Husbandman. It was Boaz in this case. It is our Heavenly Father who is the Husbandman in the other case. Secondly, we shall notice a humble gleaner. It was Ruth in this instance. It is every Believer who is represented by her—at least we shall so consider the subject. And, in the third place, here is a very gracious permission given—"Let her glean even among the sheaves, and reproach her not."

I. In the first place, then, we will consider something concerning THE GREAT HUSBANDMAN—GOD.

The God of the whole earth is a great Husbandman. In fact, all farming operations are really dependent on Him. Man may plow the soil and he may sow the seed, but God alone gives the increase. It is He that sends the clouds and the sunshine, it is He that directs the winds and the rain and so, by various processes of Nature, He brings forth the food for man. All the farming, however, which God does, He does for the benefit of others and never for Himself. He has no need of any of those things which are so necessary for us. Remember how He spoke to Israel of old?—"I will take no bullock out of your house, no he goats out of your folds. For every beast of the forest is Mine and the cattle upon a thousand hills. I know all the fowls of the mountains: and the wild beasts of the field are Mine. If I were hungry, I would not tell you: for the world is Mine, and the fullness thereof." All things are God's and all He does in Creation, all the works of His Providence, are not done for Himself, but for His creatures, out of the benevolence of His loving heart.

And in spiritual matters, also, God is a great Husbandman. And there, too, all His works are done for His people, that they may be fed and satisfied, as with marrow and fatness. Permit me, then, to refer you to the great Gospel fields which our Heavenly Father farms for the good of His children. There is a great variety of them, but they are all on good soil, for the words of Moses are true of the spiritual Israel—"The fountain of Jacob shall be upon a land of corn and wine; also his heavens shall drop down dew." God, as the great spiritual Husbandman, has many fields, and they are all fertile, and there is always an abundant harvest to be reaped in them.

One field is called Doctrine field. Oh, what large sheaves of blessed corn are to be found there! He who does but glean in it will find very much spiritual nutriment. There is the great sheaf of Election, full, indeed, of heavy ears of corn like Pharaoh saw in his first dream, "fat and good." There is the great sheaf of Preservation, wherein it is promised to us that the work that God has begun He will assuredly complete. And if we have not faith enough to partake of either of these sheaves, there is the most blessed sheaf of all—yes, it is many sheaves in one—the sheaf of Redemption by the blood of Christ. Many a poor soul who could not feed on electing love, has found satisfaction in the blood of Jesus. He could sit down and rejoice that Redemption is finished and that for every penitent soul there is provided a great Atonement whereby He is reconciled to God.

I cannot stop to tell you of all the sheaves in the Doctrine field. Some say there are only five. I believe the five great Doctrines of Calvinism are, in some degree, a summary of the rest—they are distinctive points wherein we differ from those who "have erred from the faith, and pierced themselves through with many sorrows." But there are many more Doctrines beside these five—and all are, alike, precious and all are, alike, valuable to the true Believer's soul—for he can feed upon them to his heart's content.

I wonder why it is that some of our ministers are so particular about locking the gates of this Doctrine field? They do not like God's people to get in. I believe it is because they are afraid Jeshurun would wax fat and kick if he had too much food. At least that is what I must be charitable enough to suppose! I fear that many are like the huge corn monopolist—they buy the Doctrine of Election, but keep it to themselves. They believe it is true, yet they never preach it! They say that all the distinguishing Doctrines of Grace are true, but they never proclaim them to others. There are Particular Baptists who are as sound in doctrine as any of us, but, unfortunately, they never make any sound about it—and though they are very sound when alone, they are very unsound when they come into their pulpits, for they never preach Doctrine there! I say, swing the gate wide open and come in, all you children of God! I am sure there are no poisonous weeds in my Master's field! If the Doctrine is a true one, it cannot hurt the child of God. And so, as it is the Truth of God, you may feast upon it till your soul is satisfied and no harm will come of it! The idea of reserve in preaching—keeping back some Doctrines because they are not fit to be preached—I will repeat what I have said before—it is a piece of most abominable impudence on the part of man to say that anything which God has revealed is unfit to be preached! If it is unfit to be preached, I am sure the Almighty would never have revealed it to us. No, like the old man described by Solomon, these preachers who do not proclaim good, sound Doctrine, are "afraid of that which is high." It is a mark of their senility that they fear to talk of these great things! God was not afraid to write them and we, therefore, ought not to be afraid to preach them!

The Doctrine field is a glorious field, Beloved—go into it often and glean—you may find, there, many a bushel of the finest wheat every day!

Then, next, God has a field called Promise field. On that I need not dwell, for many of you have often been there. But let us just take an ear or two out of one of the sheaves and show them to you, that you may be tempted to go into the field to glean more for yourselves. Here is one—"The mountains shall depart, and the hills be removed; but My kindness shall not depart from you, neither shall the covenant of My peace be removed, says the Lord that has mercy on you." There is a heavy ear for you! Now for another—"When you pass through the waters, I will be with you; and through the rivers, they shall not overflow you: when you walk through the fire, you shall not be burned; neither shall the flame kindle upon you." Here is another—it has a short stalk, but there is a great deal of corn in it—"My Grace is sufficient for you." Here is another. "Fear you not, for I am with you." Here is another one. "Let not your heart be troubled: you believe in God, believe also in Me. In my Father's house are many mansions: if it were not so, I would have told you. I go to prepare a place for you. And if I go and prepare a place for you, I will come again and receive you unto Myself; that where I am, there you may also be." There is the promise of Christ's glorious Second Coming and is not that a heavy ear of wheat for the Lord's children to pick up? Yes, Beloved, we can say of the Promise field what cannot be said of any farmer's field in England, namely, that it is so rich a field it cannot be richer! And it has so many ears of corn in it that you could not put in another one. As the poet sings—

> "How firm a foundation, you saints of the Lord,
> Is laid for your faith in His excellent Word!
> What more can He say than to you He has said,
> You who unto Jesus for refuge have fled?"

Go and glean in that field, Christian! It is all your own, every ear of it! Pull great handfuls out of the sheaves, if you like, for you are truly welcome to all you can find!

Then there is Ordinance field. A great deal of corn grows in that field. One part of it reminds us of the ordinance of Believers' Baptism and, verily, God's children are greatly profited even by the sight of the Baptism of others! It comforts and cheers them—and helps them to renew their own dedication vow to the Lord Most High. But I must not detain you long in this field, though it is, to many of us, a very hallowed spot. Some of my friends never go into this field at all, it is too damp a soil for them—and though the corn is very fine and very high, they are afraid to go there. Let us leave that part of the field and pass on to the place of Communion. Oh, it is sweet, Divinely sweet, to sit at the Table of our Lord, to eat the bread and drink the wine! What rich dainties are provided for us there! Has not Jesus often given us, there, "the kisses of His mouth," and have we not, there, tasted His love and proved it to be "better than wine"? Beloved, go into the Ordinance field! Walk in the ordinances of the Lord, blameless, and do not despise either of them. Keep His Commandments, for so will you find a great reward and so will He fill your souls with marrow and fatness!

But God has one field on a hill which is as rich as any of the others! And, indeed, you cannot really and truly go into any of the other fields unless you go through this one, for the road to the other fields lies through this one, which is called the field of fellowship and communion with Christ Ah, that is the field to glean in! Some of you have only run through it, you have not stopped in it. But he who knows how to abide in it and to walk about it, never loses anything, but gains much. Beloved, it is only in proportion as we hold fellowship with Christ and commune with Him that either ordinances, or Doctrines, or promises can profit us. All those other things are dry and barren unless we have entered into the love of Christ, unless we have realized our union with Him, unless we have a sympathy with His heart, unless we bear His likeness, unless we dwell continually with Him, feel His love and are ravished with His delights. I am sorry to say that few Christians think as much as they ought of this field—it is enough for them to be sound in doctrine and tolerably correct in practice—they do not think as much as they should about holding fellowship with Christ. I am sure, if they did, there would not be half so many evil tempers as there are, nor half so much pride and not a tenth so much sloth if our Brothers and Sisters went into that field more often! Oh, it is a blessed one! There is no field like that one! You may go into it and revel in delights, for it is full of everything good that the heart can wish, or the soul imagine, or the mind conceive! Blessed, blessed field is that! And God leaves the gates of that field wide open for every Believer!

Children of God, go into all these fields. Do not despise any of them, but go and glean in them all, for there is the richest gleaning in all creation!

II. Now, in the second place, we have to think and speak of A HUMBLE GLEANER. Ruth was a gleaner and she may serve as an illustration of what every Believer should be in the fields of God.

He should be a gleaner, and he may take a whole sheaf home if he likes. He may be something more than a gleaner if he can be, but I use the figure of a gleaner because I believe that is the most a Christian ever is. Some may ask, "Why does not the Christian go and reap all the field and take all the corn home with him?" So he may, if he can. If he likes to take a whole sheaf on his back and go home with it, he may do so. And if he will bring a great wagon and carry away all there is in the field, he may have it all! But, generally, our faith is so small that we can only glean—we take away but a little of the blessing which God has prepared so abundantly. And though, sometimes faith does take and enjoy much, yet, when we compare it with what there is to be enjoyed, a gleaner is the true picture of faith—but more especially of little faith. All it can do is to glean—it cannot cart the wheat home, or carry a sheaf on its shoulders—it can only take it up, ear by ear.

Again, I may remark, that the gleaner, in her business, has to endure much toil and fatigue. She rises early in the morning and trudges off to a field. If that is shut, she trudges to another. And if that one is closed, or the corn has all been gleaned, she goes to another. All day long, though the sun is shining on her, except when she sits down under a tree to rest and refresh herself a little, she still goes on stooping and gathering up her ears of corn. And she returns not home till nightfall, for she desires, if the field is good, to pick up all she can in the day, and she would not like to go back unless her arms were full of the rich corn she so much desires to find.

Beloved, so let it be with every Believer! Let him not be afraid of a little weariness in his Master's service. If the gleaning is good, the spiritual gleaner will not mind fatigue in gathering it. One says, "I walk five miles every Sunday to Chapel." Another says, "I walk six or seven miles." Very well, if it is the Gospel, it is worth not only walking six or seven miles, but sixty or seventy, for it will pay you well! The gleaner must look for some toil and trouble. He must not expect that everything will come to him very easily. We must not think that it is always the field next to our house that is to be gleaned—it may be a field at the most distant end of the village! If so, let us go trudging off to it, that we may get our hands and arms full.

But I remark, next, that the gleaner has to stoop for every ear she gets. Why is it that proud people do not profit under the Word of God? Why is it that your grand folk cannot get any good out of many Gospel ministers? Why, because they want the ministers to pick up the corn for them! And besides that, many of the ministers hold it so high above their heads that they can scarcely see it. They say, "Here is something wonderful," and they admire the cleverness of the man who holds it up! Now, I like to scatter the corn on the ground as much as I can. I do not mean to hold it up so high that you cannot reach it. One reason is that I cannot—I have not the talent to hold it up where you cannot see it—my ability will only allow me to just throw the corn on the ground, so that the people can pick it up. And if it is thrown on the ground, then all can get it. If we preach only to the rich, they can understand, but the poor cannot. But when we preach to the poor, the rich can understand it if they like. And if they do not like it, they can go somewhere else. I believe that the real gleaner, the ones who get any spiritual food, will have to stoop to pick it up—and I would gladly stoop to know and understand the Gospel! It is worthwhile going anywhere to hear the Gospel, but, nowadays, people must have fine steeples to their places of worship, fine gowns for their ministers and they must preach most eloquently. But that is not the way the Lord ordained—He intended that there should be plain, simple, faithful preaching. It is by the foolishness of such preaching that He will save them that believe. Beloved Friends, remember that gleaners who are to get anything must expect to stoop.

Note, in the next place, that what a gleaner gathers, she gets ear by ear Sometimes, it is true, she gets a handful, but that is the exception, not the rule. In the case of Ruth, handfuls were let fall on purpose for her, but the usual way is to glean ear by ear. The gleaner stoops and picks up, first one ear, and then another, and then another—only one ear at a time. Now, Beloved, where there are handfuls to be had at once, that is the place to go and glean! But if you cannot get handfuls, go and get ear by ear. I have heard of certain people who have been in the habit of hearing a favorite minister in London, saying, when they go to the seaside, "We cannot hear anybody after him. We shall not go to that Chapel any more." So they stay at home all day on Sunday, I suppose forgetting that passage, "not forsaking the assembling of ourselves together, as the manner of some is." They cannot get a handful and, therefore, they will not pick up an ear. So the poor creatures are starved and they are glad enough to get back home! They should have gone, if they could get but one ear—and he is a sorry minister who cannot gave them that! And if they got only one ear, it would be worth having. If it is only six words of God, if we think of them, they will do us good. Let us be content, then, to glean ear by ear. Let us take away a whole sheaf with us if we can, but if we cannot do that, let us get the good corn an ear at a time.

"Oh," says a friend, "I cannot hear some ministers at all! They preach such a mingle-mangle of the Truth of God and error." I know they do, but it will be a strange thing if you cannot get an ear or two of wheat, even from them! There is a great deal of straw—you are not required to take that away—but it will be remarkable if you cannot pick up an ear or two of good grain. You say, "The error that the man preaches distresses my mind." No doubt it does, but the best way is to leave the lies alone and pick out the sound Truth of God—and if there is no sound Truth in the sermon, a good plan is to read it all backwards—and then it will be sure to be sound. I heard a man of that kind, once, and when he said a thing was so-and-so, I said to myself that it was not. And when he said such-and-such a thing would happen, I said it would not—and I then enjoyed the sermon! He said that the people of God, through their sin, would perish. I had only to put a, "not," into his sentence, and what a sweet and comforting message it then was! That is the way, when you hear a bad sermon, to qualify what the preacher says. Then, after all, you can make his discourse suggest spiritual thoughts to you, and do you good! But you must be content, wherever you go to hear the Word, to pick up the corn ear by ear.

Note, next, that what the gleaner picks up, she keeps in her hands. She does not pick it up and then drop it down, as some do in their spiritual gleaning. There is a good thought at the beginning of the sermon, but you are all eager to hear another—and you let the first go. Then, towards the end of the discourse, perhaps there is another flash and, in trying to catch that, you have forgotten all the rest! So, when the sermon is over, it is nearly all gone and you are about as wise as a gleaner who sets out in the morning and picks up one ear, then drop that and picks up another. She then drops that and pick up another. She would find, at night, that she had got—what?—that she had got nothing for all her trouble! It is just the same in hearing a sermon—some people pick up the ears and drop them as fast as they pick them up.

But one says, "I have kept nearly the whole of the sermon." I am glad to hear it, my Friend, but just allow me to make a remark. Many a man, when he has nearly the whole sermon, loses it on the way home. Very much depends on our conduct on our way back from the House of God. I have heard of a Christian man who was seen hurrying home, one Sunday, with all his might. A friend asked him why he was in such haste. "Oh," he said, "two or three Sundays ago, our minister gave us a most blessed discourse and I greatly enjoyed it. But as soon as I was outside the Chapel, there were two deacons and one pulled one way, and the other pulled the other way, till they tore the sermon all to pieces! And though it was a most blessed discourse, I did not remember a word of it when I got home—all the savor and unction had been taken out of it by those deacons—so I thought I would hurry home tonight and pray over the sermon without speaking to them at all." It is always the best way, Beloved, to go straight home from your places of worship—if you begin your chit-chat about this thing and the other, you lose all the savor and unction of the discourse! Therefore I would advise you to go home as quickly as you can after the service—you might possibly, then, get more good than you usually do from the sermon and from the worship altogether!

Then, again, the gleaner takes the wheat home and threshes it. It is a blessed thing to thresh a sermon when you have heard it. Many persons thrash the preacher—but that is not half so good as threshing the sermon! They begin finding this fault and the other with him, and they think that is doing good—but it is not. Take the sermon, Beloved, when you have listened to it, lay it down on the floor of meditation, and beat it with the flail of prayer so you will get the corn out of it. But the sermon is no good unless you thresh it. Why, that is as if a gleaner should stow away her corn in the room, and the mice should find it—in that case, it would be a nuisance to her rather than a benefit. So, some people hear a sermon, and carry it home, and then allow their sins to eat it all up and thus it becomes an injury to them, rather than a blessing. But He who knows how to flail a sermon well, to put it into the threshing machine and thresh it well, has learned a good art, from which he shall profit much.

I have heard of an aged Scotchman, who, one Sunday morning, returned from "kirk" rather earlier than usual, and his wife, surprised to see him home so soon, said to him, "Donald, is the sermon all done?" "No," he answered, "it is all said, but it is not all done by a long way." We ought to take the sermon home, to do what the preacher has said— that is what I mean by threshing it. And some of you are content if you carry the sermon home. You are willing enough, perhaps, to talk a little about it, but there is no thorough threshing of it by meditation and prayer.

And then, once more, the good woman, after threshing the corn, no doubt afterwards winnowed it Ruth did this in the field, but you can scarcely do so with the sermons you hear—some of the winnowing must be done at home. Observe, too, that Ruth did not take the chaff home. She left that behind her in the field. It is an important thing to winnow every sermon that you hear. My dear Friends, I would not wish you to be spongy hearers who suck up everything that is poured into their ears. I would have you all to be winnowers, to separate the precious from the vile! With all ministers there is a certain quantity of chaff mixed with the corn, but I have noticed in some hearers a sad predilection to take all the chaff and leave the corn behind. One exclaims, when he gets out of the building, or even before, "That was a curious story that the preacher told—won't it make a good anecdote for me at the next party I attend?" Another says, "Mr. Spurgeon used such-and-such an expression." If you hear a man talk in that way, do you know what you should say to him? You should say, "Stop, Friend! We all have our faults and perhaps you have as many as anybody else—can you not tell us something Mr. Spurgeon said that was good?" "Oh, I don't remember that. That is all gone!" Just so, people are ready to remember what is bad, but they soon forget anything that is good.

Let me advise you to winnow the sermon, to meditate upon it, to pray over it, to separate the chaff from the wheat and to take care of that which is good. That is the true art of heavenly gleaning—may the Lord teach us it that we may become "rich to all the intents of bliss," that we may be filled and satisfied with the favor and goodness of the Lord!

III. Now, in the last place, here is A GRACIOUS PERMISSION GIVEN. "Let her glean even among the sheaves, and reproach her not."

Ruth had no right to go among the sheaves to glean, but Boaz gave her a right to go there by saying, "Let her do it." For her to be allowed to go among the sheaves, in that part of the field where the wheat was not already carted, was a special favor, but to go among the sheaves and to have handfuls of corn dropped on purpose for her, was a further proof of the kindness of Boaz.

Shall I tell you the reasons that moved the heart of Boaz to let Ruth go and glean among the sheaves? One reason was, because he loved her. He would have her go there because he had conceived a great affection for her, which he afterwards displayed in due time. So the Lord lets His people come and glean among the sheaves because He loves them. Did you have a rich gleaning among the sheaves the other Sabbath? Did you carry home your sack, filled like the sacks of Benjamin's brothers when they went back from Egypt? Did you have an abundance of the good corn of the land? Were you satisfied with favor and filled with the blessing of the Lord? That was all owing to your Master's goodness! It was because He loved you that He dealt so bountifully with you. Look, I beseech you, on all your mercies as proofs of His love! Especially look on all your spiritual blessings as being tokens of His Grace. It will make your corn grind all the better and taste all the sweeter if you think that it is a proof of love that your sweet seasons, your high enjoyments, your blessed ravishments of spirit are so many proofs of your Lord's affection to you. Boaz allowed Ruth to go and glean among the sheaves because of his love to her, so, Beloved, it is God's free grace that lets us go among His sheaves and lets us lay hold of doctrinal blessings, promise blessings, or experience blessings. We have no right to be there of ourselves—it is all the Lord's free and sovereign grace that lets us go there!

There was another reason why Boaz let Ruth glean among the sheaves—because he was related to her. And that is why the Lord sometimes gives us such sweet mercies and takes us into His banqueting house, because He is related to us. He is our Brother, our Kinsman, allied to us by ties of blood. Yes, more than that, He is the Husband of His Church, and He may well let His wife go and glean among the sheaves, for all she gets is not lost to Him—it is only putting it out of one hand into the other since her interests and His are all one. So He may well say, "Beloved, take all you please. I am none the poorer, for you are Mine. You are My partner, you are My chosen one, you are My bride, so, take it, take it all, for it is still in the family and there is none the less, when you have taken all that you can."

What more shall I say to you, my beloved Brothers and Sisters? Go glean, spiritually, as much as you can! Never lose an opportunity of getting a blessing! Glean at the Mercy Seat. Glean in the House of God. Glean in private meditation. Glean in reading pious books. Glean in associating with gracious men and women. Glean everywhere—wherever you go! And if you can pick up only an ear a day, you who are so much engaged in business and so much penned up by cares, if you can only spare five minutes, go glean a little—and if you cannot carry away a sheaf, get an ear. Or if you cannot get an ear, make sure of at least one grain. Take care to glean a little! If you cannot find much, get as much as you can.

Just one other remark, and then I will close. O child of God, never be afraid to glean! All there is in all your Lord's fields is yours. Never think that your Master will be angry with you because you carry away so much of the good corn of the Kingdom. The only thing He is likely to be offended with you for is because you do not take enough! "There it is," He says, "take it, take it, and eat it. Eat abundantly. Drink, yes, drink abundantly, O beloved!" If you find a sweet promise, suck all the honey out of the comb. And if you get hold of some blessed sheaf, do not be afraid to carry it away rejoicing. You have a right to it—let not Satan cheat you out of it! Sharpen up the sickle of your faith and go harvesting, for you may, if you will. And if you can, you may take a whole sheaf and carry it away for spiritual food. But if you cannot take a whole sheaf, the Lord teach you how to glean among the sheaves, even as Ruth did in the fields of Boaz. And may He, in the greatness of His Grace, let fall a few handfuls on purpose for you, for His dear Son's sake! Amen.

6
A SERMON FOR GLEANERS

"Boaz commanded his young men, saying, Let her glean even among the sheaves, and reproach her not. And let fall also some of the handfuls on purpose for her and leave them, that she may glean them, and rebuke her not."

—Ruth 2:15, 16

ALL THE WORLD DEPENDS UPON the labor of the field and the king himself is served of the plow and of the sickle. The dwellers in the country who watch the springing up of the blade through all its perils, who mark the ear as it bursts from its sheath, and who anxiously observe it until it hangs downward through ripeness and becomes yellow in the sun— these, being brought constantly into contact with clods and crops—are not able to forget their entire dependence upon the staff of life. One can hardly live where the operations of farming are carried on without often looking up to the God of Providence in anxious prayer and later, lilting up the heart in grateful praise.

But the most of us are condemned to live in this huge wilderness of bricks, where scarcely a green thing salutes our eyes. If we try to rear a plant, it is but a sickly thing, neither tempting for beauty, nor fragrant with perfume. In the absence of the bright-eyed flowers, it is small wonder if we grow a little blind towards our mother earth. We are too apt to think that we are independent of the operations of the country. That our trade, our commerce, our manufactures, are sufficient to support us. We forget, all the while, that in vain is yonder forest of masts unless the earth shall yield her fruit. In vain the emporium, the exchange, and the place of merchandise, unless the land is plowed and harrowed, and at last yields to the farmer his reward.

I would that I could recall to your memories, O you dwellers in the city, how much you depend upon the Lord God of the earth for your daily bread. Does your food fall like manna from the skies? Do you create it at the forge, or fashion it in the loom or on the wheel? Comes it not of the earth, and is it not the Lord who gives to the fertile womb of earth the power to yield its harvests? Comes not the dew from Heaven, and the sunshine from above? And do not these bring to us our bread as well as to those who abide in the midst of the fields?

Let us not forget this time of the harvest, nor be unthankful for the bounty of the wheat. Let us not forget to plead with God that He would be pleased to give us suitable weather for the ingathering of the precious grain. And when it shall be ingathered, let us not sullenly keep silence, but with the toiling workers who, well-pleased, behold the waving yellow crop, let us lift up the shout of "Harvest Home," and thank the God who covers the valleys with corn and crowns the year with His goodness.

I would order my speech, this morning, so as to act in your ears as the Harvest bell in our midland counties. I have there noticed a bell ringing early in the morning, and again towards the evening, which, I am told, is intended to tell the people the hour when they may go into the fields to glean, and when they must leave the field and go back to their homes. My sermon shall be as simple as the ringing of a bell. If it suffices to remind you of the sheaves and of the harvest, if it shall but make you thank our God who gives us the fruit of the earth, I shall be well content.

Tell me not that this is not a proper theme for the Sunday. I know you know not what you say. Did not the disciples of Jesus walk through the corn fields on the Sunday and did not the Master make the fields themselves the subjects of His sermons? I fear not His disapprobation when I say, on this hallowed day, "Lift up now your eyes and behold the fields are ripe already unto the harvest." Do you think that the outward creation is sinful and that God would be worshipped on Sundays with closed eyes and vacant faces, which must not look on flowers and fields?

There is no impurity in green grass, or flowers, or sailing clouds, or rippling waves, or ripening corn.

To the believing ear, the footsteps of the Bountiful Father are everywhere audible and the revolving seasons do but reveal the varied attributes of God. We may gather from every rustling ear a song, and listen in every harvest field to a sermon which angels might stoop to hear. It is no unhallowed theme. Come with me to the harvest field—may the Master come with us—and let us talk awhile of other things than harvests, though the harvest shall be the metaphor on which we will fashion our speech.

A word or two about the gleaning. Under the Jewish dispensation, gleaning was one of the rights of the people. The farmer was forbidden to reap the corners of the field, and if he should have left a sheaf by oversight in the field, he must not go back for it. It was to be left for the widow, and the fatherless, and the poor that dwelt in the land. No, the rights of gleaning went further than wheat and barley—the olive tree was to be beaten but once, and they were to leave the gleanings to the poor. So with the vintage. When they gathered the grapes they were not utterly to clean the branches of the vines, but leave sufficient to give a taste of the delicious fruit to the poorest of the land.

I would not have our Christian farmers less liberal under the Gospel dispensation than the farmers were under the Mosaic Law. As Boaz, in his generosity gave to Ruth more than she could legally claim, so let no possessor of the soil be questioning about the legal rights of the poor to gleaning. Let him open his gates sooner than the Jewish farmer would have done, and let him sometimes bid his men leave handfuls on purpose for the poor. Grieved am I to observe that the custom grows with many farmers nowadays to rake their fields and get all they can from the poor of the village. And I believe some would rake the stubble seven times if they could but get one ear more and leave less for gleaning.

I would not gather into my barn, were I a farmer, a sheaf, every ear of which rustled with the cries of the poor. I would not have the poor man's curse for all the rich man's field, nor make the poor dwellers in the village dissatisfied the whole year round because of a paltry handful of corn which I had added to the stock of my bursting barns. Especially you who are Christian men, I repeat it in your hearing—be not less liberal than was the Jew. And if of old, when there were types and shadows, they left good gleanings for the poor, scatter with a liberal hand now that we have come to the substance and the fullness of the Gospel. Rob not the poor man of his little, but earn his blessing by your abundant generosity in the time of reaping your fields.

I have now to invite you to other fields than these. I would bring you to the field of Gospel Truth. My Master is the Boaz. See here, in this precious Book is a field full of truthful promises, of blessings rich and ripe. The Master stands at the gate and affords us welcome. Strong men, full of faith, like reapers, reap their sheaves, and gather in their armfuls. Would you were all reapers, for the harvest truly is plenteous. But if not reapers, may you be as the maidens of Boaz. I see some servants who do not so much reap themselves as partake of that which others have reaped. I know we have many in this Church who are glad to eat the sweets, and feed upon the fat things of the kingdom, when they are brought forth each Sunday in the ministry of the Word.

But I see trembling yonder, outside the gate, a little company to whom I am to address myself today. They are not reapers, they have not strength enough of faith to take the bin sheaves. They are not as yet like household servants. They are not peaceful enough in their consciences to sit down and eat and dip their morsel in the vinegar and be satisfied. But they are gleaners, and they are saying, as they stand at the gate, "Would that I might find favor in the sight of my Lord, that I might even glean in this field, for I should then be content if I might gather here and there an ear of Gospel Grace." I am sent to you. My Master sends me as one of His young men, and thus He bids me say to you, "Come into the field and glean wherever you will, and if in the gleaning you should grow strong and become reapers, reap and carry home the sheaves for yourselves."

I. First then, like Boaz, I shall ask the question, "WHO IS THIS DAMSEL?" in order that I may find out who these gleaners are who are invited into the fields of Christ, that they may glean the handfuls that are let fall on purpose for them.

"Who is this damsel?" The first answer is, she is a Moabitess and a stranger. Ah, I know you, poor timid Heart. You say, "I am sprung of an evil stock, an heir of wrath even as others. My nature is depraved and vile. How can I hope, such an one as I am, that I should ever be allowed to go into the Master's field and glean of His good corn of Divine Grace? Oh, Sir, if you knew how I feel of my lost and helpless state! Could you but perceive how base I am in my own eyes because I have been so long a stranger to God, and an alien from the commonwealth of Israel, I think you would not invite me to glean in the field at all." Verily, my Sister, you are the very person to whom I am sent, for it was a Moabite damsel upon whom Boaz set his heart, and it was to her that he sent his message, "Abide you fast by my maidens; go not in any other field."

But I ask again, who this damsel is and she answers, "I am not only by nature a stranger but I must confess that I am now in my condition miserable and poor. I cannot buy Christ's Grace. I can do nothing to win His love. Once I thought I had some good works, but now I have none. Once I relied upon ceremonies but I have given them up, for I find no comfort in them. I am utterly poor—so poor, that I despair of ever in the future being richer than I am now. I am helpless. I am hopeless. I am nothing. Yes, I am less than nothing. Alas, I am such a miserable beggar that I am not worthy of the least of all His mercies."

Do you say this? Right glad am I, then, to hear you use such language, for unto you, again, am I sent, and unto you am I bid to give the gracious invitation—"Come into the field and glean even among the sheaves."

Now the gleaner whom I describe is not only in her own experience an alien, and a stranger—and in her own present condition naked and poor and miserable—but she has, despite all this, a decision for the Lord God of Israel. I think I hear her say, "If I perish, I will perish looking to the Cross of Christ. I have nothing of my own to bring, but I come just as I am. The Lord knows I have no other dependence but upon the blood and the finished righteousness of Jesus Christ. I forswear the gods of Moab in whom I once trusted. The world is now nothing to me. The pomp and vanities thereof have lost all their glory. As to myself, I abhor myself in dust and ashes. I would be Christ's, and if He will not have me, if I may not glean in His fields, I will never go elsewhere—

> 'If I perish I will pray,
> And perish only there.'"

It is marvelous, the tenacity with which some of these timid souls will hold to Christ. Just as a man, the more fearful he is of sinking, clutches the plank with a more terrible earnestness, so have I seen some of these fearful souls lay hold on Jesus with a grip which neither death nor Hell could unloose. Were the times of burning to come back again, many a wavering soul that can scarcely say, "I know that my Redeemer lives," would go singing to the stake! Many of those who are bold in words would prove cowardly in acts, and withdraw from Christ when it came to burning for Him. Well, it is to you that I am sent, poor timid Gleaner. Come in, come into the field, and we will see if we cannot let fall some handfuls on purpose for you.

Our description, however, is far from being complete. This gleaner is one who is exceedingly humble and self-emptied. Just observe what she says when Boaz takes notice of her—"Who am I, that I should find grace in your sight, seeing that I am a stranger?" Ah, and the woman to whom I would speak this morning has such a low estimate of herself, that when she gets a grain of hope she thinks, "Ah, it is too good for me." When, sometimes, you half hope that Christ has loved you, and given Himself for you, a sight of your unworthiness comes in and you say, "No, this can hardly be, that such an one so mean and so despicable as I, should ever be regarded by the lovely eyes of Christ my Lord."

I know you think yourself not to be pure, or fair, or lovely. And when you read such a passage as that, where Christ says of His spouse, "You are all fair, My love, there is no spot in you," tears come in your eyes, for you say, "Alas, He will never say that of me, for I am all defiled with sin, all unholy and unclean. Should He search the world through, He would not find a more worthless one than I. And should He turn the heap over again and again, he could not find one that less deserved to be the object of His pity than I, poor unworthy I."

Yes, but you are just the person to whom I am sent! Your Lord Jesus has heard of you, and He loves such as you are, for when you are little in your own eyes, then are you great in His. When you talk thus bashfully of yourself, then He loves to hear your words, for they are words of truth. In very deed, you are what you say you are, nothing but loathsomeness and corruption and depravity. And yet He who has loved you, notwithstanding all this, will never leave you till your corruption has been removed, till your loathsomeness has been washed away, till for deformity you have matchless beauty, and for unholiness His perfect righteousness. I say to you, even to you, are we sent today.

Once again, these gleaners have a very high opinion of those who are true Christians. You notice Ruth says, "I am not like unto one of the handmaidens." No, and my poor gleaner yonder, she thinks the saints of God are such a blessed people, she is not like one of them. When she gets into her sin experience she says, "If I were a child of God I should never be like this." Knowing her vileness and her imperfections she cries, "Ah, if I were one of Christ's chosen, I should be much holier than I am. Though I love His saints, I cannot dare to hope that I shall ever be numbered with them. My goodness can never reach so high as to be joined with them in visible fellowship."

Ah, I know some of you feel that if you ever did get to Heaven you would creep through some cranny in the door and hide yourselves in some mouse hole far away, where none could see you. And today, though in truth you are the best of the saints, you think yourselves the vilest of the vile. For many there are that are very rich in Divine Grace who think themselves miserably poor. On the other hand, many who say, "I am rich and increased in goods and have need of nothing," are naked and poor and miserable. Poor Moabitess, long an alien, having gone far into sin and now decided for Christ, with a sort of despairing hope that maybe He will look upon you. Today, even today, He speaks to you. Open your ears and hear Him. Forget your kindred and your father's house, for He greatly desires you, and He would have you even now come to Him and be espoused unto Him forever.

I need not prolong our description of the gleaners to whom I speak. The Holy Spirit, I hope, will find some of you out and may He press home the Truth of God to your hearts.

II. Having beckoned to the gleaner, I shall now, like Boaz, ADDRESS THE REAPERS. The ministers are the reapers, and thus speaks Boaz to them—"Let her glean, even among the sheaves, and reproach her not. Let fall some of the handfuls on purpose for her, and leave them, that she may glean them, and rebuke her not."

The first command Christ gives to his ministers is—"Rebuke her not." Ah, I fear, my Brethren in the ministry, that we have often rebuked where we ought to have comforted. And perhaps our unwise speeches, when we did not mean to do it, have been very hard blows to the afflicted in Zion. It is an ill thing for the strong cattle to push with horn and shoulder. We are very apt, unless we have much trial and trouble ourselves, to lose the lady's hand which is so necessary for a physician of souls. We keep the lion's heart but oh, the tender hand and the downy fingers—we are not so ready to keep these in dealing with sore consciences.

I know some preachers who never went to Martin Luther's school. They may have prayer and meditation, but they have never been schooled by temptation. And if we are not much tempted ourselves, if we are not emptied from vessel to vessel ourselves, we are in very great danger when we are dealing with these truths—lest we are hard with them and rebuke and reproach them, when instead we should hear the Master say—"Comfort you, comfort you My people. Speak you comfortably unto Jerusalem."

Now I take it that we do very much reproach these tender ones when we set up standards in our ministry to which we tell them they must come or else perish. Some do it in experience. I have heard old divines and, like Elihu, I have been ready to rebuke my seniors when they have taught their experience, in all its length and breadth, as necessary for all the people of God. The experience of the advanced saint must never be set up as a standard for the young beginner. There are mountains for us to climb when our bones are firm, but these mountains are not for babes. There are depths into which we are to dive when we have learned the art of plunging into them, but these are not for little children, who must be dandled on the knee and fondled at the breast.

When we describe some dark passage in our lives, and say to the young convert—"You must have felt all this or you are not a child of God," we are reproaching when we ought to have comforted, and rebuking where we ought to have consoled. So have I seen a standard of grace set up? Some Christians are eminent in their graces. Their faith is valorous. Their courage defies all danger. Their hope is bright and sparkling like a diamond. But if in our preaching we tell young converts that their graces must be equal in luster to the fathers in the Church, what do we do but rebuke Ruth when we ought to have let fall handfuls of corn for her to gather?

And so, too, with regard to doctrinal knowledge. I have known some Christians well-schooled in these matters, and deeply read in theology who, when they meet with one who knows no more than this—that he is a sinner and that Christ came to save sinners—will ask hard, wrinkled questions, which are more fit for an assembly of divines than for a babe in Christ. And because, indeed, the little child cannot untie a Gordian knot, because the babe cannot crack the hard shells of these theological nuts, they send him away and say, "The root of the matter is not in you. You have not passed from death unto life."

Oh, let us not do this, dear Brother Reapers. Let us sooner cut ourselves with our own sickle than cut Ruth with it! Let us rather be patient and very tender and receive the weak in the faith, as Christ has received them. Let us, like our Master, not overdrive the Lambs, but carry them in our bosom, and gently lead them when they need our tenderness and our care.

There is also another way in which some rebuke these gleaners, who should rather be invited and comforted—that is, by denying their faith when it is mixed with unbelief! It is marvelous, it is miraculous, that a spark of faith can live in the midst of an ocean of unbelief. You will find men who, at times, fear that they believe nothing. In their own apprehension they are so beclouded and bemisted that they have lost their way, and do not know where they are. And yet they are true Believers for all that. Some of us have passed through crisis of our being in which, if we had been asked our very name, we could hardly have told it, for we were so utterly distressed, so lost and cast away by reason of overwhelming blasphemies, or incessant temptations, that we could scarce tell our right hand from our left.

And were we therefore without faith? No, there was a little faith, still. There was an undying principle still within us when death had made us wretched men. So we must not talk to these young beginners as though the uprising of their corruption disproved the indwelling of the Holy Spirit—we must succor them. We may tell them of the dragons we have fought and the giants we have slain, but we must use discretion even in this.

And when they are in the Slough of Despond, we must not leave them to sink there up to their very necks but go lend them our hand to pull them out, for they may be in the right road even in the slough, and they may still have their faces to Zion though those faces may be besmeared with the mire and filth of that dreadful bog. Let us never rebuke or reproach these timid ones, but help and sustain them.

But further—Boaz gave another exhortation to the reapers—"Let fall handfuls on purpose for her." In our ministry there should always be a corner cupboard for the tried and timid saints. I think there should never be a sermon without a Benjamin's mess for the children. There should be strong meat for the men, but there should always be milk for the babes. Ready to adapt our ministry to all sorts of people, if we forget any, we should never forget these.

My Brothers, would you minister to these gleaners? Let me remind you, first, that our ministry most be plain, for these timid souls cannot feed on hard words. Dr. Manton once preached in St. Paul's Cathedral and a great crowd went to listen to him. A poor man who had walked fifty miles to hear the good doctor, afterwards plucked him by the sleeve and said—"There was nothing for me this morning. The doctor had preached a very learned sermon, full of Greek and Latin quotations which the poor countryman could not understand. But the doctor had not expected him and there was nothing for him."

I think there should always be in our ministry some things for poor Ruth. Something so plain and so simple that the wise acres will turn up their noses and say, "What platitudes!" Never mind, if Ruth gets a handful of corn, our Master at the last shall know who did His errand best and served Him with a perfect heart. And then, if plain, we must remember, too, that it must be very elementary. We must be often laying again the foundation stone—teaching faith in Christ again and again. As Luther says, we must repeat justification by faith every Sunday, because men are so apt to forget it.

Oh, you fine preachers who elaborate your learned essays, who work all the week long to addle your own brains and then spend the Sunday in muddling your hearers—would that you would remember these poor gleaners, who want none of your fine stuff, none of your glorious flights, none of your rounded periods! They are far better off if you will tell them that Jesus Christ came into the world to save sinners, and point their eyes to Calvary and bid them look and live. We must let fall handfuls on purpose for the weak and ignorant.

And then again, our preaching must be evangelical. Weeping eyes need Christ to dry them. Tender hearts need Jesus' wounds to make them whole. A man who lives without temptation may enjoy a Sunday's sermon without Christ in it—but give me a man who is tempted in the week and I know he wants Christ! Give me a man who has lost money in the week, or that has been subjected to ridicule for Christ's sake, and I know that you might as well offer him the husks that swine eat as offer him anything but Christ crucified visibly set forth before his eyes.

Oh, we must get back to this, all of us who are preachers! We must forget what we learned at college. We must leave behind what we pick up from learned books and come out to tell Ruth just that which she most wants to hear—that Boaz welcomes her to the field and bids her glean till her hands are full.

But then, Brethren, you will notice that these reapers were to let handfuls fall on purpose for her. Well, then, you reapers in God's field, let your preaching be very personal. Oh, I love it, when I draw the bow, not to do it at random, but to single out some troubled heart and speak to you all as though there were but one here. Not pouring the oil over the wound, but coming up to the edge of the gaping sore to pour in the oil and wine. These poor Ruths will not dare to take the corn unless we put it right in their way. They are so fearful, so timorous, that though it seems to be scattered for everybody, they think it cannot be for them. But if it is there, put there so that they cannot mistake it, then they say—"Well, that is for me. Yes, that is what I have felt. That is what I want." And they cannot, unbelieving though they are, they cannot help stooping down and picking up the handful that is let fall on purpose for them.

Then, if it is so, our preaching must always be very affectionate, for if we let fall a handful with a scowling face, our Ruth will go to the other end of the field rather than pick it up. Oh, Brethren in Christ, it is, after all, our sympathy with our fellow men which is the great engine the Holy Spirit uses in converting them. It is not merely telling out the Truth of God which is the power—God, if He had willed it, might have made statues which could preach, and they could have preached as well as we do and infinitely better if the Lord had poured the words out of their cold lips.

But he made men preachers, that men might feel for men, and that our words might come out from our hearts and so go glowing into the hearts of the afflicted. Oh, let us, then, who are reapers for Christ, be very tender with poor Ruth! And often when we forget the strong, and leave the mighty man to take care of himself, let us go to the gate to pull in the fainting Mercy and invite Christiana and her little children to sit down and rest. So would I do this morning, and therefore, I pass on to our third point.

III. As myself a reaper for Christ, I must try to follow the example of the reapers of Boaz and let fall handfuls on purpose for the gleaner. I am afraid I shall not be able to give you such handfuls as I would, but they shall come out of the right field. Oh, you timid and troubled Heart, let me drop before you now a handful of precious promises. "He will not break the bruised reed, nor quench the smoking flax."

Does not that suit your case? A reed, helpless, insignificant and weak. A bruised reed, out of which no music can come. Weaker than weakness itself—a reed—and that reed bruised! He will not break you. He who broke Rahab by His right hand will not break you. You are like the smoking flax—no light, no warmth comes from you. You are, on the contrary, like flax that smokes, giving forth a foul, offensive smell. But He will not quench you. He will blow with His sweet breath of mercy till He fans you to a flame.

Do you need another? "Come unto Me, all you that labor and are heavy laden, and I will give you rest. Take My yoke upon you and learn of Me, for I am meek and lowly in heart, and you shall find rest unto your souls." What soft words! Your heart is tender, and the Master knows it. Therefore He speaks so gently to you. Will you not listen and obey Him, and come to Him, come to Him even now? Hear him again—"Fear not, you worm, Jacob, I will help you, says the Lord, and your Redeemer, the Holy One of Israel." Or would you hear Jesus Christ speak to you again?—"Let not your heart be troubled: you believe in God, believe also in Me."

Or, again, "He is able to save unto the uttermost them that come unto God by Him." Do you not remember ten thousand such passages as these? "When you pass through the rivers I will be with you, and the floods shall not overflow you. When you go through the fires you shall not be burned, neither shall the flame kindle upon you." Or this, "Can a woman forget her sucking child that she should not have compassion on the son of her womb? Yes, she may forget, yet will I not forget you." Or this, "I have blotted out your sins like a cloud, and like a thick cloud your transgressions."

Or this, "Though your sins are as scarlet they shall be as wool. Though they are red like crimson they shall be whiter then snow." Or this, "The Spirit and the bride say, Come, and let him that is athirst come, and whoever will, let him come and take the water of life freely." Or this, "Ho, everyone that thirsts, come to the waters and you that have no money, come and eat. Yes, come, buy wine and milk, without money and without price." Oh, my Master's field is very rich. Behold the handfuls! Look, there they lie before you, poor timid Soul. Gather them up, make them your own, for Jesus bids you take them. Be not too bashful. But take them, feed on them, and go on in the strength of this meat all your days.

Well, I have dropped a handful of promises. Now let me try and scatter a handful of doctrines of grace. But Ruth starts back, for she is afraid to glean in the wheat fields of doctrine. No, but Ruth, here is the doctrine of election—come and glean that. Fear not, poor timid Soul, it is a sweet and blessed Truth of God. Hear it—"God has chosen the weak things of this world and the things that are not has God chosen to bring to nothing the things that are." "I thank you, O Father of Heaven and earth, that You have hid these things from the wise and prudent and have revealed them unto babes."

Does not that suit you, timid Soul? Are you not as a babe, as a weak thing, and as a foolish thing? Oh, there is a handful on purpose for you, in the doctrine of electing love. Hear another, the doctrine of justification by faith—"not by works of righteousness which we have done He saves us, but through Christ Jesus. We are saved through what Jesus has done on our behalf." "He that believes on Him is not condemned, but has everlasting life." What do you say? Does not that suit you? You have no good works—can you not trust Christ and His good works on your behalf? Is not this a handful on purpose for you?

"Yes but I fear," says one, "that if I were saved I should yet fall away, for I am so weak." Here is another handful for you—"I give unto My sheep eternal life, and they shall never perish, neither shall any pluck them out of My hand." "For I am persuaded, that neither death, nor life, nor angels, nor principalities, nor powers, nor things present, nor things to come, nor height, nor depth, nor any other creature shall be able to separate us from the love of God, which is in Christ Jesus."

Is not this a handful on purpose for you? "I have made and I will bear, even I will carry, even unto hoar hairs. I am He and unto old age will I carry you." What more do you want? I tell you, Ruth, there is not a single doctrine in Scripture which, if it is rightly understood, will not yield handfuls on purpose for you. Indeed, my Master's Gospel, though it is a chariot in which a king may ride, is like an ambulance used on the field of battle, in which a man with broken limbs may ride comfortably, too. Oh, it is soft riding when Christ carries in His arms! And He does this for such as you are. Broken in pieces all asunder, with your thoughts like a case of knives cutting your soul, and conscience through and through, Christ has made His Gospel to suit you.

The other day, when one of our Brothers was sick of consumption, we sent him a waterbed to rest on and the comfort it gave him was indeed delightful. But oh, Jesus Christ's bosom is something softer than that! Though you are ever so weak, though you are like a sere leaf driven in the wind and broken of the tempest, you shall yet find perfect peace and quiet in the Gospel of our Lord Jesus Christ, for it is a Gospel on purpose for you.

Once more, we have some handfuls to drop that we have gathered in another field. We have been to promise field and to doctrine field, now let us go to the field of experience. Do you not know, Ruth, that your experience is no exception to the rule? There are thousands such as you are. And I, too, who speak to you this morning, that you may know the truth of this matter, I tell you that once upon a time I stood like yourself shivering at the gate. And I said in my soul, "His mercy is clean gone forever. He will be mindful of His Covenant no more."

For years I cried for mercy but did not find it. I wrote my name among the damned and said I must perish, for God had shut up the heart of His compassion. But He has never despised the cry of His prisoner. I looked unto Him and was lightened and I am not ashamed to confess that there is light nowhere but in Him. "Oh," you say, "then your experience is something like mine!" Just so, it is. And so there is a handful on purpose for you. I know the devil tells you, you are lost in a road where Christ's mercy never travels. But it is a mistake. You are in the midst of the King's highway. I know Satan tells you that you have come to the ends of the earth. But my Lord puts it—"Look unto Me and be you saved, all you ends of the earth."

Oh, but you think you are the last man! Ah, but Christ loves to take the last and make them first, while the first he often leaves to be last. Yes, but you have written bitter things against yourself! Never mind what you have written. What a mercy it is Christ did not write them, and that, on the contrary, He has written sweet things of you! And he has said, "Return unto Me, says the Lord, for I am reconciled unto you." Soul, my Master—would that He were here to speak for Himself—for my poor words are so feeble compared with His—my Master woos you this morning.

Instead of offering you a gleaning, He offers you Himself. You came to be a gleaner. He would make you His spouse. See, Boaz comes to you. Will you have Him? The ring is in His hand. Come, stretch out the finger of your little faith and let the deed be done. Say, "Unworthy though I am, I hope, my Lord, I am Yours. No other would I have to serve, to love, to trust. Jesus, just as I am, take me and make me what You would have me to be." It is done. The marriage is ratified, and by-and-by, it shall be consummated before the eternal throne in your everlasting bliss.

I have good reason for being earnest in trying to comfort this Ruth, because, though she is a stranger, she is a sister of mine. I am a stranger, too. We both come from the same land, and the same howling wilderness. She is in trouble and my soul has known trouble, too—the same trouble-and I would desire to bring her to the port of Peace. Besides, she is to be my Master's wife, and I would be on good terms with the mistress of the house. It is ill for the reaper to have an enemy in the mistress. And since I know that this Ruth shall by-and-by find Boaz to be her next of kin, I would desire do her a good service and bring her to her Master's house, if so my Lord would honor me.

IV. I close my sermon of this morning, by stirring up timid and troubled ones to do what I know Divine Grace will make them do before long. I say, then, to you who are thus troubled in your consciences, since the field is open to you, and we bid you glean—since Boaz himself commands us to let fall handfuls on purpose for you—do your duty and be bold to believe today. You have been afraid to trust Christ up to now—trust Him now. Venture on Him. It is a poor word to use, but do it. Though something tells you you have no right to trust Christ, do it, right or not right, NOW, flat on your face before Him, with no confidence but in what He has done and in what He is doing still.

Be bold to believe in Him at this moment and you shall live. And having believed in Him, be industrious every time the Word is preached to pick up every ear of comfort in the sermon. Ruth must bend her back, though it is but one ear at a time she gathers. Think it worth while to hear a sermon in ever such a crowd, if you may get but one ear of comfort— for one ear is a great thing for one who deserves none. And but one word of mercy from the lips of Christ should be accounted more precious than rubies to a soul that deserves to hear Him say, "Depart you cursed." And when you have gathered one grain and another, seek a retentive memory to keep in your hand what you have gathered, or else you will be like a silly gleaner who stoops to glean one ear and drops another at the same time.

Carry home what of truth you can. Take notes in your heart. And when you have gathered, and your hands are full, take care to discriminate. Ruth, we are told, threshed her corn and left the straw behind—she took home the good wheat. You do the same. There is much straw in all our sermons, much that our Master would not have us say—for we are poor, poor creatures, and but fallible like yourselves. But leave the straw behind and take home the good wheat. And do us this service—do not take home the straw, and leave the wheat, as some do. There are many foolish gleaners who, if there is one word of ours awry, will tell it to our discredit—but our Master's words they will forget.

And, lastly, while you are on your knees in prayer, beating out the sermon in meditation, turn your eye to my Master. Go to Him and say to Him, "Lord, I am content to glean, though I get but one ear of mercy. But oh, that I had You! Oh, that You would give me Yourself! I have no beauty, but oh, You do not love us for our beauty but for Your beauty which You cast on us. Lord, look on me! All I can say is that if You will save me, I will praise You on earth, and I'll praise You in Heaven. There shall not be one before the Throne more grateful than I, because there shall be none who shall owe so much to Your unmerited, rich, free, Sovereign Grace."

Sinner, if you do that now, my Master will accept you. Trust Him NOW, poor Hearts, trust Him now! Away, you devil of Hell, away, away! Why will you molest these lambs? Timid and troubled consciences, hear not what your doubts and fears and Hell and the devil would say—come now to my Master! His wounds invite you—His tearful eyes invite you—His open heart bids you come. Come and trust Him, He cannot reject you if you trust Him just as you are!

God help you to do it and you shall see sin forgiven, your foes trampled under your feet, and you yourselves shall meet the great Boaz at the marriage supper and to Him shall be the glory forever and ever. Amen.

Printed in Great Britain
by Amazon